P. G.

'The ultimate in comfort reading because nothing bad ever happens in P.G. Wodehouse land. Or even if it does, it's always sorted out by the end of the book. For as long as I'm immersed in a P.G. Wodehouse book, it's possible to keep the real world at bay and live in a far, far nicer, funnier one where happy endings are the order of the day' *Marian Keyes*

'You should read Wodehouse when you're well and when you're poorly; when you're travelling, and when you're not; when you're feeling clever, and when you're feeling utterly dim. Wodehouse always lifts your spirits, no matter how high they happen to be already' *Lynne Truss*

'P.G. Wodehouse remains the greatest chronicler of a certain kind of Englishness, that no one else has ever captured quite so sharply, or with quite as much wit and affection' *Julian Fellowes*

'Not only the funniest English novelist who ever wrote but one of our finest stylists. His world is perfect, his stories are perfect, his writing is perfect. What more is there to be said?' *Susan Hill*

'One of my (few) proud boasts is that I once spent a day interviewing P.G. Wodehouse at his home in America. He was exactly as I'd expected: a lovely, modest man. He could have walked out of one of his own novels. It's dangerous to use the word genius to describe a writer, but I'll risk it with him' *John Humphrys*

'The incomparable and timeless genius – perfect for readers of all ages, shapes and sizes!' *Kate Mosse*

'A genius . . . Elusive, delicate but lasting. He created such a credible world that, sadly, I suppose, never really existed but what a delight it always is to enter it and the temptation to linger there is sometimes almost overwhelming' *Alan Ayckbourn*

'Wodehouse was quite simply the Bee's Knees. And then some' *Joseph Connolly*

'Compulsory reading for anyone who has a pig, an aunt – or a sense of humour!' *Lindsey Davis*

'I constantly find myself drooling with admiration at the sublime way Wodehouse plays with the English language' *Simon Brett*

'I've recorded all the Jeeves books, and I can tell you this: it's like singing Mozart. The perfection of the phrasing is a physical pleasure. I doubt if any writer in the English language has more perfect music' *Simon Callow*

'Quite simply, the master of comic writing at work' *Jane Moore*

'To pick up a Wodehouse novel is to find oneself in the presence of genius – no writer has ever given me so much pure enjoyment' *John Julius Norwich*

'P.G. Wodehouse is the gold standard of English wit' *Christopher Hitchens*

'Wodehouse is so utterly, properly, simply funny' *Adele Parks*

'To dive into a Wodehouse novel is to swim in some of the most elegantly turned phrases in the English language' *Ben Schott*

'P.G. Wodehouse should be prescribed to treat depression. Cheaper, more effective than valium and far, far more addictive' *Olivia Williams*

'My only problem with Wodehouse is deciding which of his enchanting books to take to my desert island' *Ruth Dudley Edwards*

The author of almost a hundred books and the creator of
Jeeves, Blandings Castle, Psmith, Ukridge, Uncle Fred and
Mr Mulliner, P.G. Wodehouse was born in 1881 and educated
at Dulwich College. After two years with the Hong
Kong and Shanghai Bank he became a full-time writer,
contributing to a variety of periodicals including *Punch*
and the *Globe*. He married in 1914. As well as his novels
and short stories, he wrote lyrics for musical comedies
with Guy Bolton and Jerome Kern, and at one time had
five musicals running simultaneously on Broadway. His time in
Hollywood also provided much source material for fiction.

At the age of 93, in the New Year's Honours List of 1975,
he received a long-overdue knighthood, only to die
on St Valentine's Day some 45 days later.

Some of the P.G. Wodehouse titles to be published
by Arrow in 2008

JEEVES

The Inimitable Jeeves
Carry On, Jeeves
Very Good, Jeeves
Thank You, Jeeves
Right Ho, Jeeves
The Code of the Woosters
Joy in the Morning
The Mating Season
Ring for Jeeves
Jeeves and the Feudal Spirit
Jeeves in the Offing
Stiff Upper Lip, Jeeves
Much Obliged, Jeeves
Aunts Aren't Gentlemen

BLANDINGS

Something Fresh
Leave it to Psmith
Summer Lightning
Blandings Castle
Uncle Fred in the Springtime
Full Moon
Pigs Have Wings
Service with a Smile
A Pelican at Blandings

MULLINER

Meet Mr Mulliner
Mulliner Nights
Mr Mulliner Speaking

UNCLE FRED

Cocktail Time
Uncle Dynamite

GOLF

The Clicking of Cuthbert
The Heart of a Goof

OTHERS

Piccadilly Jim
Ukridge
The Luck of the Bodkins
Laughing Gas
A Damsel in Distress
The Small Bachelor

Hot Water
Summer Moonshine
The Adventures of Sally
Money for Nothing
The Girl in Blue
Big Money

P.G. WODEHOUSE

Wodehouse at the Wicket

arrow books

Published by Arrow Books 2011

12

First published in the United Kingdom in 1997 by Hutchinson

Material in this anthology first appeared in the following books: 'The MCC Match', from *Mike* (1909), 'The Match with Downing's', from *Mike and Psmith* (1909, revised 1953), 'At Lords', from *Psmith in the City* (1910), 'How's that, Umpire?', from *Nothing Serious* (1950), 'Missed!' (1903), from *The Parrot and Other Poems* (1988), 'The Cricketer in Winter' (1903), from *The Parrot and Other Poems* (1988), 'The Umpire' (1906), from *The Parrot and Other Poems* (1988), 'Bingley Crocker Learns Cricket', from *Picadilly Jim* (1918).

Arrow Books
The Random House Group Limited
20 Vauxhall Bridge Road, London, SW1V 2SA

www.randomhouse.co.uk

Addresses for companies within The Random House Group Limited can be found at: www.randomhouse.co.uk/offices.htm

The Random House Group Limited Reg. No. 954009

A CIP catalogue record for this book
is available from the British Library

ISBN 9780099551362

Typeset by SX Composing DTP, Rayleigh, Essex

Penguin Random House is committed to a sustainable future for our business, our readers and our planet. This book is made from Forest Stewardship Council® certified paper.

Printed and bound in Great Britain by Clays Ltd, Elcograf S.p.A.

Contents

A Cricketing Chronology ix

Introduction 1

'The MCC Match' 53

'The Match with Downing's' 64

'At Lords' 76

'Bingley Crocker Learns Cricket' 89

'How's That, Umpire?' 96

'Reginald's Record Knock' 116

'Ladies and Gentlemen *v.* Players' 137

'Between the Innings' 152

'On Fast Bowling' 165

'Missed!' 171

'The Cricketer in Winter' 173

'The Umpire' 175

'MCC' 177

'Under MVC Rules' 178

'Five Minutes on the Cricket Field' 181

'Now, Talking About Cricket' 182

'Dulwich *v.* St Paul's' 191

Extras 195

Acknowledgements 201

Scorecards 205

Illustrations 208

P. G. Wodehouse:
A Cricketing
Chronology

1881, 15 October	– Born Guildford, Surrey
1894, 2 May	– Enters Dulwich College
,, July	– Plays for Upper IIIB *v.* Upper IIIA
1899, 20 May	– Writes first cricket match report for *The Alleynian* (Brighton *v.* Dulwich)
,, 21 June	– Plays for Dulwich *v.* MCC
,, ,,	– Takes 7/50 against Tonbridge, dismissing future Test batsman K.L. Hutchings
,, ,,	– Takes 7/13 including hat-trick as Sixth Form beat Engineers
1900, 27 June	– Plays for Dulwich *v.* MCC
,, ,,	– Takes 9/14 and 6/23 for Remove *v.* Modern VI
1900, July	– Leaves Dulwich
1900, Sept.	– Joins Hongkong & Shanghai Bank, City of

	London (plays cricket for bank teams)
1902, 9 Sept.	– Leaves bank to work as freelance writer
1903, 22 May	– First plays for Authors *v.* Artists at Esher
1903?	– First plays for *Punch*
1904 July	– First plays for Allahakbarries
1905, 29 June	– First plays at Lord's for Authors *v.* Actors
1906, 19 July	– Plays at Lord's for Authors
„ 4 May	– P.G. Wodehouse's XI plays Dulwich (team includes N.A. Knox and A.A. Milne)
1907, 15 August	– Plays at Lord's for Authors
1908, 16 July	– Plays at Lord's for Authors
1909, 15 Sept.	– Schoolboy cricketer, Mike, appears in *The Captain*
1911, 12 August	– Plays at Lord's for Authors *v.* Publishers
1912, 21 August	– Last Lord's match, Authors *v.* Publishers
1915, 15 Sept.	– First appearance of Jeeves, named after Warwickshire all-rounder Percy Jeeves
1920	– Becomes member, Surrey County Cricket Club
1932	– Founder member Hollywood Cricket Club

1939, 8 July	– Watches his last Dulwich match
1941, 21 June	– Playing cricket at Tost Internment camp, Upper Silesia, when told he is to be released
1950, 21 July	– Publishes last cricket piece ('How's That, Umpire?' in *Nothing Serious*)
1975	– Dies aged 93

Introduction

1 Dulwich Cricketing Days

Pick up the 1976 Wisden, and you find a nig-
gardly forty-four words in its obituary of
Pelham Grenville Wodehouse, recording him
as 'the famous novelist' once in the Dulwich
XI, and godfather to Mike Griffith. The 1982
Wisden has a brief review by John Arlott of
Benny Green's *P.G. Wodehouse – A Literary
Biography*, which quotes: 'In changing from
an English readership and scene to meet his
American public – in kissing cricket goodbye,
he did so only in fiction, not in life . . . passionately though he loved the game, he knew
it must be expelled from his work.'

However, for all Wodehouse and cricket
fans, it is Wisden of 1901 which is special. In
the public schools section, you will note that
N.A. Knox headed the Dulwich bowling.
Neville Knox was top-rate: a Wisden
Cricketer of the Year, he played twice for
England against South Africa in 1907, and
was called by Jack Hobbs 'the best fast bowler
I ever saw'. He was tall, loose-limbed, took a
long, angled run, and bowled at a great pace,
breaking from the off, and making the good-
length delivery rear awkwardly.

No wonder Wodehouse wrote with pleasure to a friend in 1956: 'I was in the Dulwich cricket team in 1899 and 1900, and I am always proud to think that in 1900 I used to go on to bowl before N.A. Knox (I admit he was a child of about ten then)'. As usual Wodehouse could not resist the self-deprecating touch; in fact Knox was only three years his junior, and was actually fifteen when they shared the Dulwich bowling. But it makes a better story the way he tells it.

That 1901 Wisden entry records Wodehouse's name in the Dulwich team alongside Knox. He finished last in the batting, with a total of 48 runs from ten innings (top score 14): he was primarily a fast bowler, fourth in the averages with just seven wickets at 16 runs apiece.

Dulwich were at that stage not highly regarded as a cricket school, despite producing a number of university or county players: no fewer than seven future first-class players were in the 1888 Dulwich XI. College cricketers for decades had to endure an ancient pavilion, not replaced until 1934, when the Old Alleynian the Rev. F.H. Gillingham, who played for Essex and was a pioneer of Thirties radio cricket commentary, performed the opening ceremony. Recalling pleasant associations with the game and the school, Canon Gillingham declared he was sure 'that the odours that arose from the subterranean passages, which were known by the name of "changing rooms" had been of great service in preparing him for his work in the slums'.

The college in Wodehouse's day did boast an Old Boy as England captain, the shadowy

M.P. Bowden, who was just seventeen and still at Dulwich when he first played for Surrey in 1883 as a stylish wicket-keeper batsman. He toured Australia with Vernon's team in 1887-88, and a year later went to South Africa as deputy to C. Aubrey Smith. When the future film star took ill with fever on the eve of only the second Test to be played against South Africa, Monty Bowden deputised: at the age of 23 years 144 days, he remains the youngest to lead England. Bowden settled in South Africa, first working in partnership with Aubrey Smith on the Johannesburg Stock Exchange, but then he came on hard times, tried smuggling liquor, and in 1892 died in Rhodesia after a fall, aged only twenty-six.

On 2 May, 1894, Wodehouse started at Dulwich, where his older brother Armine had studied before him. Dulwich then had 600 boys: he spent the first term living at the East Dulwich home of an assistant master. When the new school year began in September, he became a boarder in Escott's House. (He had a brief spell as a day-boy when his parents took a house nearby: he then resumed as a boarder, this time at Treadgold's House). He was already known as Plum to his family, although simply Wodehouse (Minor as long as Wodehouse Major – Armine – was still there) to masters and classmates. Later he recalled: 'If you say Pelham quickly, it comes out sounding something like Plum. I rather liked it, particularly after I learned during my boyhood that a famous Middlesex cricketer, Pelham Warner, was called Plum. He captained England a number of times'.

The junior Wodehouse was encouraged in

all things by his father – not least in his cricket (although Ernest Wodehouse was no athlete): a nephew, Norman Wodehouse, captained England at rugby in the Edwardian age, but otherwise the only sporting successes of the immediate family were P.G. Wodehouse's older brother and Dulwich trailblazer Armine, to a modest degree, and then Plum, himself. According to Richard Usborne, there was a scale of reward for the Dulwich sons – five shillings for taking six wickets, ten shillings for making fifty, and so on. We might feel six wickets to be a greater achievement than half a century – but those generally low scores in turn-of-the-century cricket may explain the ratio, and Dulwich had a name for unhelpful wickets on which batsmen could struggle for success.

The first record of cricketing activity for young Wodehouse is in the college magazine, *The Alleynian*, of October, 1894: he appeared for Upper IIIB against UIIIA in July. It was not a match of high achievement, as his team made 39 and 49, edging home by three runs, to 53 and 32. Wodehouse batted No.11, recording a pair of ducks – bowled by H.A. Green in both instances. He did not bowl, but took a second innings catch.

One other future author of potential cricket significance was in full flow for the College that season, described in *The Alleynian* as 'a very promising slow bowler, with a good legbreak, a useful though not a stylish bat, and a good field'. This was Hugh de Selincourt, whose evocative novel on between-the-wars village cricket, *The Cricket Match*, set at Storrington in Sussex, which was to be published thirty years later, still stands as the best single work of fiction the game has inspired.

It is not until 1899 that Wodehouse becomes a figure of cricketing note – or at least, that his senior cricket is properly recorded at all. He won his 3rd XI cap in 1898: next season saw only one old 1st XI cap return, and the young fast bowler made the jump to the Firsts – effectively replacing brother Armine, who had been in the Eleven for the previous two years. In a school of 600 boys, a place in the First XI was something special.

In June of that year Wodehouse appeared as cricket writer for the first time, reporting four games played by Dulwich against other schools (in which he of course took part). He was in his customary batting slot of last man, and the Brighton match report informs us: 'Wodehouse now came in and held us in suspense for about a quarter of an hour, hardly a run being added'. In fact he shared one of the best stands of the innings – all of 11.

The older Wodehouse then returned to face his brother. Dulwich played Oxford's Corpus Christi College, Oxford, with Armine Wodehouse batting No.5, and probably involved in arranging the fixture. For the school, Wodehouse Minor managed a single wicket, and his favourite score: nought not out. Dulwich recorded just 101 against 287 by the undergraduates.

Then came opportunity, and triumph: 'Wodehouse bowled excellently throughout the innings, taking seven wickets for 50 runs', reads the account of Dulwich, well beaten by Tonbridge. Oh yes – with another Wodehouse duck. In this match, he secured his most glorious scalp – having the aggressive but graceful Kenneth Hutchings caught for 60. Sixteen at the time, Hutchings was an outstanding schoolboy cricketer who went on to play for Kent and seven times for England. Like so many of the best cricketers of the late Victorian and Edwardian age, he was to die on the battlefields of France.

The season ended with the final Cup match in which the Sixth Form beat the Engineers – this time bringing glory. Wodehouse not only took 7/13, including the hat-trick, as the Engineers chased a mere 80 in the second innings (having made 191 in their first innings): he actually hit 24 not out. *The Alleynian* wrote a famous summary widely recorded by his biographers: 'Wodehouse bowled well against Tonbridge but did nothing else. Does not use his head at all. A poor bat and very slack field'. It is a stern verdict, but appears to be fair enough – and intriguingly, all the indications are that Wodehouse wrote it himself.

By 1900, in his final year, Wodehouse had not advanced from No.11, but he did have a significant No.10 ahead of him – N.A. Knox, whose career has been recorded earlier. His great achievement with the ball came for the Remove in June, against Modern VI, when he missed by a whisker the bowler's Holy Grail of ten wickets in an innings. He dismissed the first nine batsmen – eight bowled, one lbw – before a change bowler in Ransford pinched the No.11: Plum's figures were 9/14 off 23 overs, with nine maidens. He also took 6/23 off 17.5 overs (five maidens), to give him a remarkable match analysis of 15 wickets for 37 runs – not to mention making 20 and 14.

Dulwich massacred Brighton, beat Tonbridge easily, drew creditably against Corpus Christi – and then we have for the first time a sight of the marvellous Wodehouse literary style (the report is unsigned, but there can be little doubt of the author).

This was College *v.* Masters, reported for *The Alleynian* with comments such as: 'Messrs Doulton and Douglas began treating the bowling in an indecently frivolous manner, with fours and other varieties in abundance'.

The Masters made 127, and the School replied: 'With the last man but one in, we had a margin of five runs. Then the telegraph [scoreboard] began to show an unaccountable flippancy at such a crisis. First it encouraged us with a score of 124, then when we were not looking, it changed to 127. Despair reigned supreme. Suddenly back it went to 126, and as the last man fell at that score, we thought we had saved the match. But before we reached the pavilion, 127 was again registered, and the most the frenzied team could do, was to do for the scorer – a congenial task, and neatly carried out'. Wodehouse made his usual duck, but was beginning to find his metier.

The Alleynian summed up his career in that farewell season: 'A fast righthand bowler with a good swing, although he does not use his head enough. As a bat, he has very much improved, and he gets extraordinarily well to the pitch of the ball. Has wonderfully improved in the field, though rather hampered by his eyesight'.

MCC included Dulwich in its school

matches in the Wodehouse years: on 21 June, 1899, the college played host to MCC & Ground (i.e. the visitors including professionals from the Lord's ground staff, primarily to do the hard work of bowling, while the MCC amateurs could enjoy themselves batting).

This match was inconclusive: Dulwich made 99 and MCC 101, the College batting again for 4/74: Wodehouse at No.11 was bowled for his usual duck by the Kent professional G.G. Hearne (an all-rounder who played one Test in South Africa in 1891-92) – and took no wickets.

A year later MCC made 200, with Wodehouse getting two wickets: the college scored 7/135, and he did not bat. The most notable member of the visiting team, which included seven past or current first class players, was the lordly K.J. Key, who skippered Surrey from 1894 to 1899, and would certainly have been an heroic figure to Wodehouse, who was a Surrey supporter.

Despite these contacts, Wodehouse did not become an MCC member. It was not until 1920 that he joined a first-class club – and then it was Surrey, rather than MCC or even Middlesex. He remained a member for just four years, alongside his brother Armine: Surrey's home ground, The Oval, was where Wodehouse watched most of his first-class cricket.

He shared a study and dormitory at Treadgold's for 14 months, from May, 1898, with Bill Townend, a friend and regular correspondent for the rest of his life, who also was intent on making a living as a writer (to much good advice and occasional more practical help from Wodehouse). The choice of house and housemaster may have been a factor in developing the Wodehouse love of cricket: J.G. Treadgold had been master in charge of Dulwich cricket since 1876, and he had done much to put the game on an efficient and whole-hearted basis.

Given his enthusiasm for Dulwich cricket and its cricketers, it is ironic that the last direct Wodehouse involvement with the 1st XI was to prove a doleful occasion. In *Performing Flea*, Townend records the final Wodehouse visit to Dulwich and England. 'In the latter end of July, 1939, Plum was over briefly from Le Touquet, where he lived, and on the Saturday he and I went to Dulwich together to see the school play St Paul's, and it was the dullest cricket match, the slowest and most uneventful that either of us had ever seen. I said goodbye to Plum at about 4 o'clock, and left him seated in the pavilion, looking rather bored and rather disconsolate. That was the last time I saw him. Six weeks later, war was declared.'

In *The Alleynian* of the same month, Wodehouse described this, his last Dulwich match as 'This frightful game, probably the dreariest ever seen on the school grounds'. But in the contradictory fashion of cricket, the Dulwich XI of that year achieved considerable success and fame, with Trevor Bailey and A.W.H. Mallett its stars, although the St Paul's XI is forgettable and forgotten.

Wodehouse's report includes the much-quoted reference, 'Bailey awoke from an apparent coma to strike a four'. Trevor Bailey, the finest modern player to come from

Dulwich, can laugh at this today, but at the time was rather hurt: in 1994 he recalled that he felt it a little unfair as 'I had quite a good match' (he took five wickets and made 41 not out in the single innings game).

However Bailey knew of the depth of Wodehouse devotion to Dulwich and its cricket from the previous season, when at 14 years of age, he had been a member of the 1st XI which went through unbeaten. Captain A.C. Shirreff recalled how Wodehouse responded to the achievement: 'He sent me what he termed "a purse of gold to buy bats with" – it was a five pound note actually, and we went to the Palladium and had a meal with it, and I still had change.'

Wartime distance and disruption did not erode the Wodehouse nostalgia for his school, or his interest in its students. On 22 April, 1945, he wrote to Townend from Paris to say he had been sent Dulwich Year Books for 1943 and 1944, 'which I was delighted to have, though it was saddening to see the Roll of Honour. Quite a few of the names were of chaps I knew slightly as members of the cricket and football teams. I see a fellow named Darby who was in the cricket team of 1935, and wrote to thank me for a notice I gave him of my report of the Tonbridge match.

'By the way, was 1944 a very wet summer in England? I ask because that was the year we won all our seven school cricket matches, and the lad at the head of the batting averages has an average of 25. We seem to have outed the opposition for about 83 and then to have made 84 for eight ourselves. The top score seems to have been 60. Very odd'.

May 22 brought a Wodehouse declaration that he was 'in a state of suspense, wondering if Billy Griffith is playing for England in the Test at Lord's. The Paris *Daily Mail* gave the list of the team, and said: "Either Griffith or Evans will keep wicket." The report of the first day's play merely gives the score, and today's paper does the same, plus a description of the Australian innings. I am going down to town this afternoon in the hope of finding an English paper. I am hoping that Billy got in all right.'

That Old Alleynian and long-time Wodehouse friend (although 33 years his junior), Lieut. Col. S.C. 'Billy' Griffith did indeed make his representative debut, taking four victims, but failing with the bat and unable to prevent Lindsay Hassett's Australian Services XI from winning by six wickets what was officially not a Test, but a 'Victory Match'.

In 1950 Wodehouse wrote to Townend of chairing the Old Alleynians dinner in New York, attended by ten ex-Dulwich students – it was a joy, he wrote, to discuss matters such as whether it was 56 or 65 that R.J. Jones made against St Paul's in 1911. (This may be a rough recall of R.K. Nunes, the first West Indies Test captain, in England in 1928, who topped the 1911 Dulwich batting with 770 runs at an average of just under 60).

Memory may have been fallible – but affection for the old school, its players and its times, was constant and everlasting.

One final pointer to the hold of Dulwich for its most romantic Old Boy is recorded in the college history, *God's Gift*. A Wodehouse letter explained how he once gave up the chance of earning an estimated 50,000 dollars by writing the lyrics for a musical 'because the cable putting up the offer arrived just when the Dulwich team was going great guns, and I couldn't bring myself to miss the Haileybury match'.

2 Post-Dulwich: Player and Enthusiast

Suddenly Dulwich days were at an end, and like his schoolboy hero Mike (who had expected to go to Cambridge), Wodehouse was deprived of an anticipated Oxford place, primarily because his father's finances had fallen away. The departing student had worked hard for a classics scholarship to Oriel College, but had to drop out before sitting the exam. In September, 1900, a few weeks before his nineteenth birthday, he was engaged by the Hongkong and Shanghai Bank in Lombard Street, in the heart of the City of London's financial district.

Freelance writing had already begun in February with his first paid contribution, an article in *The Public School Magazine*: 'Some Aspects of Games Captaincy' brought half a guinea. (The author had not enjoyed any captaincy experience at anything, but here as throughout his writing, shrewd observation and readiness to venture served him well).

But if Wodehouse soon convinced not only himself but also his superiors that he was a misfit as a bank clerk, then he fitted well enough into bank social life, where – again as with Mike – his colleagues were public school men of his own vintage and interests. He joined the bank rugby and cricket teams: a picture is preserved showing the young Wodehouse suitably stern in rugger kit, although no-one has found any similar record with the bank XI.

London bank cricket was becoming increasingly well organised in Edwardian times, all the major banks owning well-appointed grounds in the outer suburbs. The Hongkong and Shanghai had facilities at Beckenham, now used by the Midland Bank. But sadly there is no sign of any Hongkong and Shanghai match records from Wodehouse's time. The one cricketing record is of Wodehouse as spectator rather than player – a spectator at one of the great matches in Test history.

Ronald Mason in his collection of essays, *Sing All A Green Willow*, writes of Wodehouse the bank clerk cutting across the river Thames to The Oval for a long lunch-hour whenever so inspired, and being there on Wednesday, August 13, 1902, the last day of the final Test against Australia – immortalised as 'Jessop's Match'.

This was 'a rainy, disappointing morning', with England set nearly all day to make 263 – and Wodehouse, one eye on the clock because of that lunch-hour, watched the fall of three batsmen for 10, and two or three overs later, 'the temporarily merciful interruption of a shower'.

Jessop survived with Jackson to lunch and five wickets down – 'and with who knows what temptations tearing him in twain, the young P.G. Wodehouse turned his back on The Oval, and went back to the Hongkong and Shanghai Bank'. Mason records the sequel – how Jessop stormed to the most spectacular hundred in the history of the Tests (he hit 104 out of 139 scored while he was at the wicket, reaching three figures in 75 minutes), and Hirst and Rhodes saw England to one-wicket victory as the light worsened and steady rain set in.

'And while these Olympian and indelible deeds were being enacted, the young P.G. Wodehouse ground resentfully at his ledgers in the bank. He could not have known of what he had missed until, at the very earliest, late that same evening. Possibly not even until next morning, there being no BBC then. And when he did get to know, what a bewildering conflict in his loyal enthusiast's mind of pride in the achievement, and regret at his own loss . . .' Within a month, Wodehouse was to walk out of the bank for good.

The original account of the Wodehouse visit comes in A.A. Thomson's *Cricket My Happiness*, published in 1952, in which the author recalls Wodehouse telling him what he had seen, and missed. 'The story of Jessop's match has been recalled many times, but I set it down here once more for a particular reason', Thomson writes. 'The game was a triumph for England, but fifty years later, I have heard of a tragedy, minor but poignant, connected with it'. He records how Wodehouse – 'the greatest English humorist since Dickens' – dashed from the City to The Oval 'instead of having any lunch, and saw Jackson and Jessop start their stand. He did not even take time to buy a sandwich.

'Alas, when Jessop had made 39 (this was

at lunch), poor Wodehouse had to go, for time and tide and the Hongkong and Shanghai Bank wait for no one. "I always remember" he told me, "how formidable Trumble seemed that day. One got the feeling that he was unplayable. And the wicket was in a terrible state by that time . . ."'

Thomson understood what it meant for a true cricket-lover to miss such an historic climax. 'Seeing Jessop make 39 not out of that immortal 104, and not being there at the most dramatic finish in history, must have been like seeing Ellen Terry in the first act of *Romeo and Juliet*, and then having to leave the gallery because your nose was bleeding. If that had happened to me, I should never have smiled again. It just shows that a noble spirit cannot be quelled . . .'

And so, after two years of banking (and apparently erratic cricket), Wodehouse resigned his post on 9 September, 1902, so that he could concentrate on freelance writing. Cricket now became something he had to seek out for himself – but if the freelance needed to devote his energies to earning a living rather than relaxing, there was always plenty of cricket for the public school man in those Edwardian days.

Although now fully embarked on his writing career, Wodehouse in his cricketing aspirations fell between two great literary teams. He was too young to have more than brief involvement with J.M. Barrie's Allahakbarries, and was long settled in America when Sir John Squire's Invalids made their name in the Twenties, inspiring that epic of a village match against eccentric

London visitors, in A.G. Macdonell's glorious *England, Their England*.

Barrie founded the Allahakbarries in 1887 (he explained the name was derived from the Arabic invocation 'Allahakbar', which he claimed meant Heaven help us; a more accurate translation is simply 'God is Great'). The first match was a challenge to the Surrey village of Shere where Barrie had walked for years, and their initial foray at the wicket produced just eleven runs. This was hardly surprising, as a couple of his players had never previously held a bat, and had to be instructed on their way to the ground.

The fun of that unique chance to 'exhibit their skill or incompetence, and to regain their youth', under Barrie's irresistible chiding and charm, kept the team going almost until the First World War swept away innocence. Barrie was still to turn up in distinctive team blazer and cap for a match in 1913, aged fifty-three, although the 'real Allahakbarries' had ended in 1905.

Wodehouse is thought to have played a few games with Barrie's bizarre mix of authors, artists, actors and other artistic lights: he was introduced in July, 1904, by *Punch*'s Owen Seaman, to open the batting at the Black Lake cricket week. But the Allahakbarries were by now beginning to run out of a little steam because of alternative interests, and the passage of the years.

The only known scorebook of this curious team is Barrie's own book for the seasons 1899-1903, recorded mostly in near-illegible pencil, and held in the MCC Library: Wodehouse had not at that stage made his appearance. Two privately circulated booklets were produced by Barrie on his colourful elevens, but these appeared in 1893 and 1899, when Wodehouse was still a schoolboy, so he is not part of the Allahakbarrie official record.

Wodehouse also enjoyed what should have been much more light-hearted cricket, but quite possibly was more serious – playing at Emsworth House, the preparatory school where his friend Herbert W. Westbrook was an assistant master. On the border of Hampshire and Surrey, the village had a name which was put to good use soon enough: Wodehouse stayed there for six months from January, 1903, on excellent terms with the headmaster, Baldwin King-Hall, who shared his lodger's enthusiasm for cricket. Wodehouse recalled: 'We used to play cricket against various teams on the ground, though it was really much too small for grown-up cricket.'

In August, 1903, Wodehouse was named fulltime assistant to Harold Begbie on the *Globe* 'By The Way' column, and had to return to London. This involved a couple of hours urgent work each morning, after which he could turn to other writing. He recalled: 'I'd walk back to my lodgings and more or less start work right away, doing short stories and things. I played a certain amount of cricket, and I never really wanted anything to do, I was so keen on my work.' From around 1903 he played occasional cricket with a *Punch* XI under the guidance of Owen Seaman, the classicist who edited the humorous magazine in its great days, and later introduced him to J.M. Barrie. He was always on the lookout for the promising writer who could play cricket.

In Edwardian England, the well-connected cricketer simply assembled his own invitation XI when he felt like a game: on 4 May, 1907, P.G. Wodehouse's XI returned to Dulwich to play the College. The visitors included the unreliably ambitious Herbert Westbrook, a teacher with visions of being a writer, with whom Wodehouse was to collaborate for a decade (and upon whose erratic lifestyle the feckless but immortal Ukridge is based). Also playing was the cricket essayist E.V. Lucas – and a rising young writer named A.A. Milne. Then twenty-five, Milne played much club and social cricket around London, and wrote charmingly about his team, 'The Rabbits'.

But the stars of yesterday did not shine at the old school: neither Wodehouse nor his one-time pace partner Knox got a wicket – and the boys won comfortably.

Wodehouse had first taken his own XI back to Dulwich in 1904, and continued the fixture until 1908, as well as appearing at least four times with the Old Alleynians. He also played with three other invitation teams; the F.P. Knox XI, the J.M. Campbell XI and the F.D. Browne XI. In his last fixture against Dulwich in 1908, Milne played again, while the twenty-six-year-old Wodehouse recaptured something of his youth by picking up three wickets.

Even though writing about cricket had gradually overtaken actual playing well before his thirtieth birthday, Wodehouse did achieve every cricketer's ambition, appearing at Lord's not once, but six times.

On 29 June, 1905, when the young free-lance writer was not quite twenty-four, he played for Authors *v.* Actors – one of a series of modest-level matches for which the head-quarters of cricket was regularly made available (the main ground, at that: the Nursery ground, then known as the practice ground, was not used for matches until after World War Two).

Sir Arthur Conan Doyle captained the writers, who included Cecil Headlam, J.C. Snaith, Albert Kinross, Horace Bleakley, Major Philip Trevor and E.W. Hornung. Doyle was an excellent club player who represented MCC regularly: Wisden said of him, 'though never a famous cricketer, he could hit hard, and bowl slows with a puzzling flight'. He is notable in cricket records for having captured just one first-class wicket in his career – for MCC *v.* London Counties, on 25 August, 1900, when he dismissed none other than W.G. Grace.

If Doyle was the Authors' star, several others had fair cricketing reputations. And E.W. Hornung was the creator of Raffles, the gentleman thief who used his cricketing credentials to wangle his way into country houses where he switched to cat burglar, lifting jewellery and valuables from bedrooms at dead of night. Hornung, married to a sister of Conan Doyle, was a keen player, but had not made the Uppingham XI.

Doyle's was a useful team in the social game of the day, but the Authors, after making a modest 149 on debut, were toppled by the Actors, thanks to a thunderous unbeaten century by one V. O'Connor.

Wodehouse opened the batting with his skipper and duly made his regulation duck – bowled by C. Aubrey Smith, who at 41 was fully fast enough to worry the occasional player. The Actors needed only twenty-five overs to score 156 for just three wickets. But Wodehouse then got some revenge. His ten overs may have cost him an expensive 58 runs, but he bowled H.B. Warner, and caught Aubrey Smith. (Warner was to join Smith in Hollywood and make his name in cinema history playing Christ in the 1927 de Mille Biblical epic, *King of Kings*).

A year later the Authors squared accounts by 24 runs: Wodehouse's batting ability was perhaps better suited to No.9 (where he made a significant 14) and he bowled only in a light-hearted second innings, to pick up three cheap wickets.

The 1907 match saw Wodehouse, again at nine, score just a single, in a total of 193, and then pay out 36 runs in five overs for two wickets: the Actors scored 4/253 for comfortable victory.

In the following year, the English weather caught up with the fixture; just five overs were bowled in 1908 – with Wodehouse down on the batting order at No.11. He did not return to Lord's until 1911, when the opponents were the Publishers: he took four wickets, all bowled, in a score of 240, and made a notable 60, promoted to No.4, in a drawn total of 218 for 8. And finally in 1912, Wodehouse at No.6 made 27 out of 206, before rain again intervened and the match was abandoned with just seven more overs bowled.

Writing to his friend Leslie Havergall

Bradshaw (to whom *Psmith in the City* is dedicated, and who was then working in New York), Wodehouse explained: 'I made 27 in seven minutes for the Authors at Lord's before being stumped, and then rain stopped play. Last Saturday I got 50 for our village, and took seven wickets. We had to run everything out, and it nearly killed me. With boundaries, I should have made a century.'

He was thirty, and although he took regular exercise then as he did throughout his life, anyone who has ever both batted and bowled for any length of time at any level will understand his weariness – especially on that oddity of the age, a ground without boundaries.

The Lord's occasion was the last Authors' match – and really the end of serious cricket for the increasingly diverted Wodehouse. But one other noteworthy author crossed his path around this time in a bizarre cricketing context. H.G. Wells invited the young Wodehouse and a number of other writers to dinner and, as Wodehouse recalled years later: 'We had barely finished the initial pip-pippings when he said, apropos of nothing: "My father was a professional cricketer". If there's a good answer to that, you tell me. I thought of saying, "Mine had a white moustache", but finally settled for "Oh, ah", and we went on to speak of other things'. (Joseph Wells, father of H.G., had played seven matches for Kent in 1862-63).

Albert Kinross, a dramatic and art critic, wrote in his autobiography, *An Unconventional Cricketer*, an account of E.W. Hornung's establishing the Authors team, which played first at Esher. Early Authors' elevens included the Hampshire player H.V. Hesketh-Prichard as star bowler. Another celebrity was the novelist A.E.W. Mason who 'did not appear to take the game very seriously'. Kinross wrote: 'P.G. Wodehouse, I remember, joined us, an old Dulwich boy, and still rather the schoolboy. He, as Lucas before him, was doing comic stuff for *The Globe*. Esher, then something like a village, put us up and fed us; its ladies turned out for tea with us on the field; and in the evening there were dinner-parties'.

He explained that 'in addition to our games at Esher, we sometimes went to Lord's and did battle with teams of Actors and Publishers. Needless to say, St. John's Wood was not blocked with traffic on these occasions, though the Actors proved something of an attraction. Far more so than we poor Authors, who were so misprized that one charitable firm of batmakers arrived with the offer of a guinea weapon to the one of us who should make top score. Neither Doyle, nor Hornung, nor any of us leapt at it, exactly'.

Kinross pays tribute to Conan Doyle as an inspiring captain, who 'usually delivered the goods, made runs, took wickets, and held catches'. But the Publishers 'were not so good a side, and we beat them easily – although in S.A. Pawling of Heinemann's they had one uncommon bowler who could send down a fast in-swinger with an authentic fizz – a brute of a ball to start on, and bad enough at any time'.

The Artists had been less famous: in cricket terms, the most significant of the first team was Albert Chevallier Tayler, whose general work is overshadowed by his 1905 series of forty-eight drawings, 'The Empire's Cricketers' – now very much a collector's item. *Cricket*, the weekly journal which ran from 1882 to 1913, records the Artists in their Edwardian heyday as fairly basic in organisation: the only subscription payable was life membership, at one guinea.

The first Esher match against the Authors (tagged 'E.W. Hornung's XI') was on June 30, 1902. It was on 22 May, 1903, that twenty-two-year-old Wodehouse made his debut. Batting at No.4, 'J.G. Wodehouse' made 33 before being run out – at twenty-two he must have been fit enough to take quick runs, especially against the mainly middle-aged opposition, so you can only speculate that he may have been let down by his more elderly partner, either Kinross at five, or Conan Doyle himself, who made 28 at No.6.

The Authors made a solid 184: the Artists were dismissed for 83, with J.C. Snaith taking six wickets, including that of Chevallier Tayler for a duck.

On 20 May, 1904, Wodehouse was relegated (if the *Cricket* report can be believed) to last man in a 12-a-side match, scoring 44, while his No.11, P. Graves (brother of Robert Graves, the poet), made 55 not out, to give the Authors a total of 221. The Artists were dismissed for 159: Conan Doyle took five wickets, and Hesketh-Prichard six. There was an intriguing, distant echo of that match and the Wodehouse part in it when on 26 September, 1960, he wrote to Graves in response to a letter, commenting how nice it was to hear from him 'after all these years. I remember so well the time – gosh, it must be nearly fifty-five years! – when we shared rooms . . . I remember that stand in the Artists match. Great days!'

Kinross in 1923 was the only survivor of the pre-war Authors to play a further match when a few enthusiasts at the Authors' Club challenged the Actors – 'who seemed to have gathered new strength', as he records. 'Young Alec Waugh did his best, but we hadn't a chance'.

It was Waugh who in the Wodehouse compilation, *A Centenary Celebration*, published in 1981, records: 'I first encountered Plum Wodehouse in August, 1910, [it was actually the 1911 match] at Lord's, where he was playing cricket for the Authors against the Publishers. I remember the match well. Conan Doyle captained the Authors, S.S. Pawling the Publishers. Pawling, universally called "The Skipper", was one of the bulwarks of the Hampstead CC, which was known as the nursery of Middlesex cricket: he had played a few times for Middlesex' (three matches in 1894).

Waugh recalled 'a closely contested draw' (the Authors lost 8/218, chasing 240). 'My score card, which I kept for many years, is now in the Haverford College Library. Hugh de Selincourt was playing, as was Gunby Hadath whose name was as well known to readers of *The Captain* as Plum's.

'I can remember nearly everything about the match except Plum's own innings. He went in first wicket down [second wicket, says the MCC match list] and made sixty runs. I can only assume it was a sound, straight affair.'

Those Wodehouse Lord's appearances were among his last direct cricketing involvements of any sort: there followed a steady physical distancing from the game over a long period, embracing war, vast social change, marriage, and his discovery of America, which led him virtually to settle there from 1911, with only the periodic return visit to Britain.

3 The Cricket Writings

P.G. Wodehouse, freelance writer of the new Edwardian era, drew on his public school experience to write public school stories very early in his career – and also drew on his cricketing experience to weave cricket into those stories, and write other studies, mostly humorous, on the game.

His first (unsigned) article on cricket published by *Punch* in 1902 was tantalisingly titled, 'Under M.V.C. Rules'. This, as his official biographer Frances Donaldson commented, 'combines the style of *Punch* in the early years with the style we are now able to recognise as that of Wodehouse, to a remarkable degree. It is a comment on a newspaper article about a new game called vigoro, which is said to have characteristics of both cricket and tennis, to be played with a soft rubber ball, and to be playable all the year round by both sexes'. The title is at first sight a mystery – until you realise that for Marylebone Cricket Club, the author wishes you to read 'Marylebone Vigoro Club'. (See 'Under MVC Rules', page 178).

The first Wodehouse book, *The Pothunters*, also published in 1902, records life at St.Austin's, but has no cricket content: it is not till we progress a year to *A Prefect's Uncle* that the game appears. A focus is Beckford *v.* MCC – with a pleasant essay about life in the classroom on the day of a school match, boys trying all sorts of dodges in the effort to monitor the progress of play from indoors. There is a leisurely and extremely readable account of the match, with Wodehouse taking us inside the mind of the cricketer – and it is much as it would be today.

The other school stories – *Tales of St Austin's* (1903); *The Gold Bat* (1904); *The Head of Kay's* (1905); and *The White Feather* (1907) – contain little cricket. *Tales of St Austin's* does offer in 'The Odd Trick', a fascinating insight into the realism of the young Wodehouse about the morality of cricket – both the public principles of the game, and the ruthless manner in which it can be exploited by the unscrupulous or mischievous. It tells how irreverent Philip St H. Harrison, punished for 'ragging' by prefect Tony Graham, takes his revenge when dragooned into umpiring a house match. Twice he gives a batsman 'Not Out' to Graham's bowling: once he calls a 'no-ball' to invalidate a legitimate delivery about to break the wicket.

The droll tale, 'How Pillingshot Scored', tells of an imaginative junior who escapes inevitable humiliation and dire punishment in a feared Saturday examination, by the simple expedient of volunteering to score for the XI at an away match on that day, his form-master admitting he had been personally scored off by this trick.

The St Austin's collection includes 'The Tom Brown Question', which first appeared in *The Public School Magazine* of December, 1901 – only months after the young Wodehouse left Dulwich. This is another sample of Wodehouse's realistic approach to school life, involving a sly assault on the 'wholesome' public school stories of the day which earnest adults sought to foist on their juniors, as a character analyses *Tom Brown's Schooldays*. He cites the instance where Tom's school (Rugby) plays MCC. Tom wins the toss on a plumb wicket – and puts the visitors in first. 'Now, my dear sir. I ask you, would a school captain do that? I am young, says one of Gilbert's characters, the Grand Duke, I think, but, he adds, I am not so young as that. Tom may have been young, but would he, *could* he have been young enough to put his opponents in on a true wicket when he had won the toss?'

Wodehouse briefly turned ghost in 1907, when he wrote for his old Dulwich teammate N.A. Knox an article, 'On Fast Bowling', published in the *Daily Mail*. This was Knox's finest season, when he played twice for England against South Africa, making him a good by-line for Britain's first truly popular newspaper. Sporting heroes were greatly to its taste; the Knox article appeared on 17 May, sandwiched between 'England through Japanese eyes' (an account of how he found life in Britain by Mr K. Jugimura, a special correspondent of the Tokyo daily *Asahi*); and a study: 'Colonial Conference reports – Mr Winston Churchill and the *Daily Mail*'.

The partnership makes for very much a period piece, but begins in undoubted Wodehouse style: 'Pace is to a great extent a gift, like red hair, or collecting postage stamps'. It ends with a boost for an unnamed but identifiable brand of dry ginger ale, at which manufacturer Cantrell & Cochrane was so pleased that it had the article reprinted in a four-page pamphlet.

In 1909 Wodehouse produced one of his most intriguingly different books – a broad satire called *The Swoop, Or How Clarence Saved England*. This was a caricature of a genre increasingly popular as Edwardian Britain became concerned about potential invasion. It tells of Clarence Clugwater, a Boy Scout of ingenuity, determination, and impeccable loyalty, who rallies a shaken Britain when that unaware nation is invaded by Germany, Russia, Switzerland ('the Swiss Navy bombarded Lyme Regis'), and five more countries.

"Paper, General?"

Clarence's self-centred family, to his patriotic despair, is quite unaware of the threat posed to England by avaricious outsiders. His oldest brother Reggie, reading his paper, comments that Fry is on his way to his eighth successive century, and wonders if he goes on like this, might Lancashire win the championship? 'I thought he was playing for Somerset', comments younger brother Horace. 'That was a fortnight ago – you ought to keep up to date on an important subject like cricket', says Reggie.

In 1909, we have Wodehouse forecasting an era in which cricketers would coolly shrug off loyalties and change counties – something increasingly happening today, if not quite yet at the mid-season speed he envisaged. Clarence ultimately restores Britain to the control of her own people, in the process making Kennington Oval safe for Fry, and whoever else may have been lately acquired by Surrey.

The Captain ran a series of Wodehouse cricket stories and articles, beginning in 1902: by 1909 the style and name were well enough established to justify four contributions to a Newnes anthology, *Twenty-five Cricket Stories*. 'Tom, Dick and Harry' is a Wodehouse theme used later – that of two contestants for a maiden's hand, agreeing that the one who makes more runs in a village match shall be allowed a clear sight of the quarry, only to find afterwards that she is already engaged (in this case to the curate who captains their side). 'The Wire-Pullers' is rare as a Wodehouse story told in the first person by a girl – a seventeen-year-old whose father reluctantly promises to let her holiday in London if he scores 50 in the next village match – and the young lady finagles that happy outcome. The supposed author is Miss Joan Romney, who appears again in three similar stories, using her feminine wiles to sway the results of games, ranging from a village match played to decide whether a right-of-way shall remain open, to Gentlemen *v.* Players at Lord's. (English cricket today might yearn for such an effective seductress.)

'The Lost Bowlers' tells of a modest touring team discovering that a crack eleven of first class cricketers has been assembled to meet them in the final match of their Devon tour. They hijack the players (and win) by the simple expedient of luring them into a brand-new, fascinating motor car – remember this was 1909 – and driving them off into the distance on the pretext that no-one knows how to turn or stop the monster.

Another outlet for early Wodehouse was the monthly magazines which entertained the middle and better-educated lower classes. *Pearson's* of August 1906 ran 'The Pro', a curious Wodehouse story leaving you to work out the validity of the plot. The basis is that an Oxford star drops out of the amateur game to play under an assumed name as a Middlesex professional.

Hired by a financier to reinforce his country house eleven in a significant match, Gray the pro. tells his temporary employer he will ensure they win only if allowed to marry the man's daughter. The father consents, and all is well – except that the cricket buff can only be alarmed at the account of how the couple had become betrothed 'during the luncheon interval of the third day of the 'Varsity match in the little balcony at the top of Lord's pavilion. His reason for selecting this spot was that he knew it would be empty at that time'. It may well have pleased Wodehouse to cock a snook at Lord's authorities, who still allow no women in the pavilion except for the Queen.

But much more factual is an intriguing indication that intrusive tabloid journalism poking its nose into the private lives of cricketers is not only a creation of vulgar today. When Desmond Fendall folded his lady in his arms, this was noticed by an acute newspaperman. He 'wired an account of the incident to his journal, which came out that evening with the following headlines:

The Lady at Lord's
Tender Interlude at 'Varsity Match
Did she Accept Him?
Amorous Oxonian Pops in Pavilion

Pearson's of 1909 published the heart-warming tale of 'Reginald's Record Knock', which explains how his kindly teammates reward their excellent but inept friend Reginald Humby for his qualities by allowing him one magical day of success on the field. The introduction explains him: 'Reginald Humby was one of those men who go in just above the byes, and are to tired bowlers what the dew is to parched earth at the close of an August afternoon. When a boy at school he once made nine not out in a house match, but after that he went all to pieces.'

The stories clearly split into two distinct

groups – one in which the cricket itself is the prime topic, and the result either for team or individual, is the key to the tale and its climax; and a number in which romance is linked in some way to a match or the performances of those involved.

But from this stage it was less and less the English market that lured Wodehouse's ambitions, and books, short stories and articles aimed at the affluent American publishing world increasingly took over, with only occasional references to cricket. A virtual farewell to the game is made in mid-Atlantic, so to speak, with the 1917 appearance of *Piccadilly Jim*, set both in New York and London, as Wodehouse sought to link the two settings to produce a story marketable in both countries. This offers the trauma of Bingley Crocker, a small-time American actor required to live in London, where in place of his beloved baseball, he is offered the inexplicable substitute of cricket.

Newly acquired butler Bayliss is called in to explain cricket, and we are offered a masterly display of incomprehension between the cricket-aware servant, unable to appreciate that his master is baffled, and the same master, struck almost dumb that anyone should consider this strange pastime as any substitute for his ball game. Bayliss ploughs on helpfully, seeking to explain a scorecard, while in response Bingley Crocker uses breakfast table implements to explain baseball (as Basil Radford and Naunton Wayne did for cricket in the Hitchcock classic, *The Lady Vanishes*).

Cricket was to make one other substantial but untypical appearance in the 1950 collection of short stories, *Nothing Serious*, and the tale: 'How's That, Umpire?' (See page 93). This offers a sharp slice of social comment, in a dispute as to whether wasps are harassing the somnolent inhabitants of the Lord's pavilion. A man in a walrus moustache is drawn into the debate: he insists there are no wasps around – 'Not in the pavilion at Lord's. You can't get in unless you're a member'.

Precisely.

4 Mike

The outstanding Wodehouse cricketer and cricket character is Mike Jackson, so sharply etched that just the name 'Mike' immediately identifies him for the cricket enthusiast who knows his Wodehouse. The author Alec Waugh wrote in his autobiography, *Myself When Young*: 'the only great cricket story of recent times is a school story – P.G. Wodehouse's *Mike*'. And Malcolm Muggeridge recalls in his autobiography, *The Infernal Grove*, how he introduced Wodehouse to George Orwell in Paris in 1944: 'They just talked cricket' [Orwell knew the game from his Eton days]. The two of them got on very well . . . Orwell and I talked a lot about Wodehouse later, and I mentioned, as an example of how very little writers can judge their own work, that Wodehouse had told me he considered his best book to be *Mike* – an early and surely immature schoolboy story. Of it, Wodehouse told me – in all seriousness, too – that the book had captured the "ring of a ball on a cricket bat, the green of the pitch, the white of the flannels, the cheers of the crowd", or words to that effect. "Certainly," said Orwell to my immense surprise. "Wodehouse is perfectly right. Mike is certainly his very best book.'"

Mike appeared in a serial in *The Captain* from April, 1907. The original title, 'Jackson Junior', was changed when the tale appeared in 1909 in book form, to the more familiar *Mike*. This incorporated the second Mike story, published in *The Captain* from April, 1908, as 'The Lost Lambs'. By 1953, the two were to be published separately once again, this time as *Mike at Wrykyn*, and *Mike and Psmith*.

Mike is a younger son of a prosperous family with three first class cricketer brothers – Joe, a Test batsman, Frank and Reggie, lesser county lights; Bob is in his last year at Wrykyn, three years older than fifteen-year-old Mike. Arrived at Wrykyn, Mike gets an early chance to show his quality when 1st XI captain Burgess bowls to him in the nets.

He is 'saddened somewhat' when his stumps go flying, second ball – but he keeps out the remaining deliveries, thanks the captain, and is given the accolade: 'You don't run away, which is something'. Mike 'turned purple with pleasure at this stately compliment' – and today's cricketer should realise that Mike, facing a well-built and genuinely fast bowler aged eighteen or nineteen, is put to the test wearing by modern standards, minimal protection. There is an echo of this required toughness in Edwardian public school cricket in another story, featuring Clephane, an outrageous fast bowler who is unplayable one day, and impossible the next. Allocated the worst possible pitch in a vital house match, he terrifies the opposition, his first ball bringing a delicious response. 'The batsman observed somewhat weakly – "Here, I *say*!", and backed towards square leg. The ball soared over the wicket-keep's head, and sped to the boundary. The bowler grinned pleasantly'.

It is a nice reminder that modern cricketers may wince at the sight of West Indian short-pitched tactics, but the amiable Wodehouse, ninety years ago, was quite happy to record schoolboys facing ferocious attacks, on extremely dangerous wickets, with minimal protection – and with no thought that it might be 'not cricket'.

Mike becomes Wrykyn's star bat, spending three years in the 1st XI and doing everything right on the field – but nothing in the classroom to suggest he is benefitting from his studies. So he is removed to a smaller school, Sedleigh, which has a reputation for scholastic achievement – and bitterness at losing his chance to skipper Wrykyn in his last year is brought out to excellent effect in the second part of the saga.

At Sedleigh Mike meets his lifelong friend Psmith, just transferred from Eton by his own father; Psmith is also a cricketer of quality, but a lazy one, in line with his brilliant character overall. The pair finish up playing for their new school and setting it on the path to a bright cricketing future.

Mike Jackson returns in *Psmith in the City*, required to make a living in a City of London branch of the New Asiatic Bank, increasingly confused by his duties, and wondering about an alternative future, when it is decided for him. Brother Joe phones one morning to ask if

Mike can play for the county at Lord's at short notice.

He scores a splendid century (see 'At Lord's', page 73), and fellow-banker Psmith, having persuaded his father to watch Mike, is able to suggest that the wealthy Psmith Senior fund both of them in going to Cambridge.

We jump another season to *Psmith, Journalist*, which explains how, after their first Cambridge year, Mike, having hit a century in the Varsity match, tours the United States with an MCC team (Psmith 'had played cricket in a rather desultory way at the University'). After scene-setting events, Mike has to leave with the team for Philadelphia – which shows that Wodehouse knew his American cricket, this city then being the strongest cricketing base of the States.

By the time of *Leave It to Psmith*, in 1923, we learn that Mike saw out his Cambridge days (regrettably with no further cricket details), married, and became agent to the Psmith estates – only for Psmith Senior to die, and the estate to be broken up. Mike is offered the chance to buy a farm, and the book turns on the convoluted efforts of helpers to obtain the money.

The Mike saga is unusual in that certain specific details are carefully updated in later editions. When Jackson Junior made its debut in *The Captain* in 1907, the Jackson family scan morning papers (no radio, let alone TV, of course) to see what progress has been made by the three cricketing brothers. They learn for instance if 'that ass Frank had dropped Fry or Hayward in the slips before he had scored'.

At Wrykyn, Mike's new friend Wyatt

inquires of him: 'Are you a sort of young Tyldesley, too?' Wyatt explains after nets that if you showed captain of cricket Billy Burgess 'N.A. Knox bowl, he'd say he wasn't bad'. Arguing for Mike's inclusion in the XI, Wyatt urges Burgess, 'here's this kid waiting for you with a style like Trumper's'. And when Wrykyn play Ripton, with a legspinner opening the bowling and doing instant damage, a Wrykyn player asks: 'I wonder if the man at the other end is a sort of young Rhodes, too?'

Twenties editions were unchanged – but by 1953 for *Mike at Wrykyn*, and *Mike and Psmith*, amendments had become essential. Frank this time has dropped Sheppard or May; Mike is a sort of young Compton; Trueman has replaced N.A. Knox; Mike has a style like Hutton's – and the other bowler is envisaged as a sort of young Tattersall.

Mike's cricket career may have fizzled out with the distraction of marriage and the restrictions of poverty – but his name lives on. When Wodehouse's Dulwich friend 'Billy' Griffith had a son in 1943, he was not merely to become Wodehouse's godson, but was christened 'Mike', rather than Michael, in deliberate tribute.

In middle age, Mike Griffith wrote: 'Being christened Mike has its drawbacks, especially with solicitors and legal documents, when nobody will take my word for it! I am of course thrilled to have an association with PG – incidentally I took on Grenville (his second Christian name) later on, and have passed this name down to my son. PG's letters are wonderful. I never met him, alas. My father visited him in Remsenburg, Long Island, but I never did so, more's the pity. My own career as a county cricketer for Sussex was fairly undistinguished, but PG was always interested in my exploits'.

The original edition of *Mike* is now so scarce an item (a first edition was quoted recently at £1,200) that it is perhaps no surprise that even Mike Griffith has only a second edition, in his personal 'super collection of PG'.

5 Jeeves (and Bertie)

The one specific cricketing reference and reminder that lives on throughout Wodehouse, despite the fact that its subject has nothing whatever to do with the game, is in the naming of Jeeves. He was christened after Percy Jeeves, the Warwickshire professional who was killed in France in 1916. Jeeves the cricketer fitted into the persona of Jeeves the gentleman's personal gentleman for his immaculate turnout and behaviour: records of the time indicate that he was renowned for impeccable grooming, spotless flannels, and smartly ironed shirts.

A rare photograph shows Percy Jeeves looking much more the Edwardian amateur than a paid servant of the county – strong features, confident half-smile, blazer collar turned up, white cravat tied stylishly.

A Yorkshireman, born at Earlsheaton, Jeeves grew up in Goole: he made his debut against the Australians in 1912 while qualifying for the county, but had only two seasons to show his skills before enlisting. F.R. Foster described him as 'the greatest all-rounder in the game in 1914': he turned out for The

Players against the Gentlemen at The Oval – and was memorably termed 'one of the most gentlemanly of Players'. Plum Warner was much impressed with his 4/44 off 15 overs, predicting he would be an England bowler soon. He was quickish medium, with an easy action, getting much life off the pitch.

The *Goole Times* in a feature on that district's favourite son, almost certainly was misguided when it suggested that Wodehouse spent some time at Edgbaston in 1913-1914, seeing the young Jeeves in action: there is no record that he ever went to Birmingham. In 1960 Wodehouse wrote to a correspondent to recall watching a county match at Cheltenham, 'when one of the Gloucestershire bowlers was called Jeeves. I suppose the name stuck in my mind, and I named my Jeeves after him'.

A Gloucestershire bowler? Well – from 1913 to 1960 is a considerable stretch of memory. It was probably on August 14th-16th 1913, when Gloucestershire beat Warwickshire by 267 runs, Jeeves making one run and taking only one wicket, but picking up two catches – perhaps pocketed so silently and smoothly that the action instantly reminded Wodehouse of his noiseless and efficient new manservant character (who first appeared in print in 1916 – only a matter of weeks after the original Jeeves died on the Somme).

A visit to the cricket museum set up in 1993 at Edgbaston under the direction of curator Ken Kelly reveals a mini-display of Percy Jeeves, with a *Yorkshire Post* article on 1981 by the cricket writer Rowland Ryder, under the evocative headline: 'What-ho, Jeeves – the demon bowler'.

Ryder tells the story of Percy Jeeves, and records writing to Wodehouse in 1967 to check if cricketer had indeed led to valet. Wodehouse replied from Rensembrink on October 26, 1967 – the letter is on show – to confirm the link, mentioning the Cheltenham match and saying: 'I remember admiring his (bowling) action very much'. Percy Jeeves's county cap, and pictures of the promising player in action, add to the display.

Ryder in his semi-autobiographical *Cricket Calling* (1995), devotes a chapter to 'The Unplayable Jeeves', recording how his father when Warwickshire secretary had spotted the unknown Jeeves in a village match, was impressed by his 'effortless grace' as a bowler – and invited him to join the county.

For those who had long felt that the original Jeeves deserved some more lasting memorial in the game he played so briefly, there was good news when Wisden in 1996 at last listed Percy Jeeves in its historic record of 'Births and Deaths'.

So that is cricket and man (although Wodehouse decided not to invest his Jeeves with the cricketing quality of the original): what of cricket and master? Sadly, there is no record that Bertie Wooster ever trod the cricket field; he was a racquets Blue, played a little tennis – and that appears to be that.

The inimitable quality of Jeeves and his master is borne out by the very modest attempts to copy these stories – even by those well-qualified to do so. The quirky Simon Barnes of *The Times* produced in 1989 a lively series of cricket studies in the styles of noted authors. *A La Recherche du Cricket Perdu* includes: 'How's That, Jeeves?' This is clever in being quite true to the original style, but even the ingenious Barnes found it impossible to conjure up a true Wodehousean plot: the story casts Jeeves as Loamshire dressing-room attendant, looking after county skipper Wooster in the Benson & Hedges semi-final against Surrey, and suggesting at a crucial moment that Gussie Fink-Nottle bowl his leg-breaks. Gussie has apparently achieved nothing in other matches despite persistent self-belief that he is a slow bowling genius: why he should now prove unplayable, taking seven wickets for ten runs, is unexplained. But as Madeline Bassett, bizarrely transmogrified into telephonist at Loamshire, renews her tryst with hero Gussie after having threatened to hitch up with Bertie, and Loamshire chef Anatole decides against joining Surrey when his fiancée Pamela from behind the members' bar changes her mind about a transfer because of Surrey's defeat, Jeeves has once again given satisfaction.

6 The American Years – Cricket Endures

In a 1975 BBC interview, Wodehouse declared: 'My game now is baseball. Oh, I'm crazy about it. I'd much rather watch a baseball game than a cricket match. I think what's wrong with cricket, that is, if you're keen on one team – I was very keen on Surrey – well, I'd go to see Surrey play say Lancashire, and I'd find that Lancashire had won the toss, and they'd bat all day, whereas with baseball, the other side only bats about ten minutes at the most.'

Wodehouse in America obviously enjoyed

little immediate exposure to cricket: his friends were mostly Americans, and his writing was aimed at a market which would have been baffled at more than the occasional glancing reference to so alien a game.

There were brief refresher courses in cricket on the fairly regular prewar London visits: Wodehouse tried to watch Dulwich play either cricket or rugby whenever he returned, and in 1932 he contributed to *The Alleynian* an account of Dulwich at home to Tonbridge. This is very much a standard cricket report of its age, offering no humour: only the initials at the end identify the author.

But the report ran to nearly 2,000 words, and was written at the height of Wodehouse's earnings capacity on either side of the Atlantic. He was then able to ask – and get – as much as 4,000 dollars for a contribution to the *Saturday Evening Post*. By 1935 he was down to just a thousand words on Dulwich *v.* Tonbridge. Again the style is very simple, with no indication of batting or bowling method, tactics or detail, such as we expect today. But the reports were written out of love and loyalty, and at some financial sacrifice.

Meanwhile cricket continued to slip into the professional Wodehouse product, as in *Laughing Gas*, published in 1936, when Reggie, third Earl of Havershot, mourns his translation under the bizarre influence of dentist's gas into the body of the juvenile screen idol, Joey Cooley. The young peer grieves for many reasons, not least the loss of his notable physique: 'I used to go in for games, sports and pastimes to a goodish extent, thus developing the thews and sinews. What future have

I got with an arm like that? As far as boxing and football are concerned, it rules me out completely. While as for cricket, can I ever become a fast bowler again? I doubt if an arm like this will be capable of even slow, leg-theory stuff. It is the arm of one of nature's long-stops. Its limit is a place somewhere down among the dregs of a house Second Eleven.'

These are cricketing deep waters: slow leg-theory was known to the young Wodehouse, but confused in the English mind of 1936 by fast leg-theory – a very different and fishy kettle.

Bodyline was a major concern to cricket of the Reggie Havershot year, as the England team headed for Australia, uncertain of its welcome after the bitterness of 1932-33. (This was when England won back the Ashes with the aid of ruthless fast bowling tactics directed by skipper Douglas Jardine, the supremely skilled Harold Larwood bowling intimidatory deliveries that brought Australia's batting genius Don Bradman down to mere mortal proportions). Did Wodehouse simply wipe that sour episode out of his mind?

Certainly he must have known all about it: friends kept him informed on the game, and he still saw English papers. He was to have a unique opportunity to learn about this controversial episode in 1937, when the fast bowler Gubby Allen, a member of the Bodyline team, returned from leading England in the 1936-37 Ashes series via America, spending some time in Hollywood, and having much to do with Wodehouse.

But remoteness from regular cricket news caused Wodehouse some problems in understanding changes in the country of his birth and youth. Based in endlessly affluent America, he found this new Britain a strange place. In 1946 he wrote to Townend: 'Clothes must be the devil of a business in England. How do cricket pros manage about white flannel bags?'

There was social change in the English scene as well. In the mid-Fifties he wrote to a friend: 'I say, what's happened to English cricket? I understand there aren't any amateurs any more. They pay people like Cowdrey? I wonder how that's arranged, and how much they get. In my day the Fosters . . . I never understood how all of those brothers played first-class cricket all summer, every summer. Except Basil, of course. He was the actor. And the Gilligans and Crawleys and Ashtons. If I came back to England in the summer, I wonder if I'd find cricket interesting.'

But if Wodehouse with his new love of America and his focus on the American market was a long way from his beloved Dulwich, then cricket in a sense had long ago come to him. As sound galvanised the motion picture industry in the Thirties, Hollywood became a marvellous market for English actors with smooth accents.

By 1932 there were so many Englishmen – many of them public school products – in films, that they decided to introduce the natives to cricket, and have fun playing it themselves. At that year's inaugural meeting of the Hollywood Cricket Club, Wodehouse –

who had settled there on a lavish contract to MGM as a screenwriter – took the minutes, offered to help buy equipment, and inevitably renewed acquaintance with the club's guiding spirit.

This was the imperious Charles Aubrey Smith, his old opponent of Authors *v.* Actors days a quarter of a century earlier: twelve years later he was to be knighted for services to acting – not least his standard and effective portrayal of the British stiff upper lip.

The Hollywood CC diamond anniversary book in 1992 reflects the tidal wave of change in the club from those distinctive and fairly elitist Thirties origins, when it was run by and for upper middle-class – if sometimes slightly raffish – English actors. Today it is dominated by hardworking Asian business and professional men, determined to continue the tradition established by Aubrey Smith with colleagues such as Errol Flynn, Nigel Bruce, Boris Karloff, Herbert Marshall, George Arliss, H.B. Warner, Frank Lawton and David Niven. Sir Laurence Olivier himself played just once, and Cary Grant was a postwar patron.

The book reproduces a 1937 fixture list, with Pelham Wodehouse recorded as a vice-president along with Ronald Coleman, Leon Errol and George Arliss. Wodehouse is listed as paying 100 dollars to become a life member. But there is no record that he ever actually played: by 1932, at fifty-one, he accepted that his cricketing days were well past (only to be revived in the improbable wartime setting of Tost internment camp eight years later).

While Charles Aubrey Smith, former

England captain as he was, held the limelight for decades as the grand old man of the Hollywood CC, another club member had special links with the world of Wodehouse.

He was the fearsome Boris Karloff – in reality the kindliest of men – who was born down the road from Dulwich at Camberwell in 1887, when Wodehouse was six. He learned his cricket at Uppingham, and threw himself delightedly into the new club – even having 'Hollywood Cricket Club' emblazoned on the tyre cover of his car.

When Gubby Allen visited Hollywood on his way home from the 1936-37 series in Australia (which he lost so memorably after winning the first two Tests), Aubrey Smith called the England captain into the Hollywood team a couple of times. A match against Pasadena saw Hollywood reinforced not only by the current England skipper, but also by one of twenty-five years earlier. The omniscient C.B. Fry was a brilliant scholar, who represented England at cricket and soccer. Pasadena fielded while Allen scored 77, Fry got 12 – and David Niven made 15.

Wodehouse spent much time with the visitor, as he recorded in a letter to Townend: 'I have been seeing a lot of Gubby Allen, who came from Australia via Hollywood. A very good chap. I met him two years ago at Le Touquet. He was extraordinarily interesting about body-line, and the picture he drew of conditions during the Jardine-Larwood tour were almost exactly like an eyewitness's description of the Spanish war.

'Larwood apparently was going about saying that he did not intend to return to England without having killed at least a couple of Australian batsmen, and Jardine threatened to leave Gubby out of the team if he would not promise to start bowling at the batsmen's heads immediately he was put on.

'This tour appears to have been almost as bad, in a quieter way. Apparently the Australians never cease trying to slip something over on the English captain. Example – in the NSW match one of the umpires, named Barlow, cheated so badly that Gubby told them that he would never play with him again. A few days passed, and the time arrived for the umpires for the Test Match to be submitted to Gubby. He had some difficulty in getting them to name them, but eventually they said they would be two men named Jones and Bartlett.

'"Bartlett?", said Gubby. "I've never heard of him". "Oh, very well-known Australian umpire", they replied. "Excellent fellow, and very kind to his old mother". "You don't by any chance mean that fellow Barlow, do you?" said Gubby. Upon which, the Australian Board of Control slapped its forehead and said: "God bless my soul, isn't it amazing how one gets names mixed up. Yes, Barlow, of course. That's the chap's name". The idea being that if Gubby had accepted Bartlett and agreed to Bartlett, it would have been too late for him to have done anything when he arrived on the field for the Test Match, and found Barlow grinning at him.

'Gubby struck me as a bit soured by it all. He was also sick with the rank and file of the English team, who failed enthusiastically on every occasion, so that the fast bowlers had to get the side out of the hole in practically every game. What England needs apparently, is the sort of bowler I used to be in my prime – the sort of man who never gets a wicket, but bowls six yorkers per over, and can't be scored off.'

However, that enticing tale about disguised-but-rejected umpire Andy Barlow, who stood in eleven Tests between 1931 and 1951, and was widely regarded in Australia as a first rate official, is not confirmed. He did not officiate in either of two MCC-NSW matches of 1936-37 – but he did so in the two Victorian games against the visitors, in November and February. Was he – even under the pseudonym of Bartlett – actually nominated for a Test? There is no record of it – and to complicate the story just that touch further, there was no umpire Jones in Australian cricket at that stage, either.

There was an umpire J. Bartlett in Australia – a Queenslander, who in 1932-33 handled a single Sheffield match, and did not cross MCC paths.

All five Tests of 1936-37 were umpired by E.G. Barwick and J.D. Scott, so that the suspicion remains that Wodehouse wrote a pleasingly entertaining, recollected-in-tranquillity-but-not-actually-spot-on report of what the England skipper told him.

Wodehouse had recorded an early bodyline tour impression in a letter to Townend of 4 January, 1933, when he commented: 'Second Test Match. How about it? What a bunch of rabbits! Isn't it odd how cricketers during the county season seem such marvels, yet no good in Australia.' In fact, England swept to a crushing 4-1 series victory in that turbulent season.

One disappointment for the historian is that Wodehouse was not present from 25-28 August, 1932, when an Australian team led by the veteran spin bowler Arthur Mailey played four one-day matches against Hollywood. The locals batted 20 men in the first game, and 18 in the others: the tourists won each convincingly, with the young (and honeymooning) Don Bradman making 83 not out in the first match.

In 1965, the Wodehouse interest in cricket was stimulated by a parcel of books from John Arlott, and he promptly responded to say they were 'a welcome addition to my cricket library. I gulped them all down at one go, and particularly enjoyed the Maurice Tate one.'

In a sign of the sharp eye he still kept on the game, the letter of thanks added: 'The prospects in Australia don't look very bright, though I remember everybody said that P.F. Warner's side hadn't a chance. You never know what will happen out there'. Warner's team, which upset the critical applecart, had won 3-2 in Australia in 1903-04, and the memory was clearly still significant for his namesake.

7 The Cricket Record

Given that cricket played so substantial a part in Wodehouse's life, it has received surprisingly modest attention beyond a series of thoughtful references by Benny Green in *P.G. Wodehouse – A Literary Biography*. The only specific study appears to be that by Jim Coldham in *The Cricketer* magazine of 27 June, 1953.

Assessing Wodehouse as cricketer and cricket writer, Coldham stressed that unlike many writers of fiction, he wrote with a considerable knowledge of the game. He summarised the Dulwich career, with the odd aberration of referring to his 'slow bowling'. Wodehouse is on record as bowling slow leg-breaks – but this was at age 59 on 21 June, 1941, in the unlikely setting of Tost internment camp, in Upper Silesia. He joined enthusiastically in the impromptu and ill-equipped matches the internees played, to the puzzlement of their guards and non-English prisoners.

Wodehouse later noted this as his first game for twenty-seven years, which means he had not played since 1914, the year he turned thirty-three. 'I found sailors playing cricket in the yard – real bat and stumps (ball made by the sailors, interned from the captured S.S. Orama). I hadn't played for twenty-seven years, and found it hard to get down to balls. I bowled and got one wicket – great fun'.

He explained how the ball tended to get through the barbed wire surrounding the yard, whereupon 'a sailor is shoved through after it'. Another entry in his camp diary explained how they played on a dirt pitch with a pump just where the bowler ran in. 'If the ball goes through the barbed wire, we have to tie two bats together with a handkerchief and grope for it. If it goes out the other end, the sentry prods it back with a bayonet'.

One final question should be asked about Wodehouse the sportsman: might he have made the grade as a first class cricketer at Oxford? The truth is probably that he was never more than a moderate player: an immediate pointer is that his older brother, Armine, always regarded as the better of the two, was apparently never in the running for a Blue.

E.A. Wodehouse did no more than secure a regular place in his college XI, after having an early opportunity in the Oxford Freshmen's Match of 1900. He failed to take a wicket, made only four not out, and seven, and dropped out of contention. Among his mostly anonymous teammates was one who four years later not only won the deciding Sydney Ashes Test for England with a spell of five wickets for 12 runs, but did so with the aid of his revolutionary bowling style that was to make him a major figure in cricket history. This was B.J.T. Bosanquet, first practitioner of the googly, or wrong 'un – also called the bosey, in honour of its inventor.

Wodehouse would have had to earn his Blue as a fast bowler: in his favour, he would have been up at Oxford presumably in 1901, when the university bowling was 'unreasonably bad', according to Geoffrey Bolton in his history of the Oxford University CC. Bolton records that 'things went badly for Oxford cricket in the next six years' (1902-07), so an eager and successful Wodehouse might well have forced his way into an unsuccessful team.

But ambition might have been lacking: his determination to be a writer was so ingrained when he left Dulwich, that it seems unlikely that he would have devoted himself to cricket sufficiently to impress his potential skipper.

The point is made today by Wodehouse's step-grandson, Sir Edward Cazalet (son of

Wodehouse's step-daughter Leonora), who after World War Two periodically visited Wodehouse in America, when the pair would cheerfully talk cricket, past and present.

'He understood the game to a T – and he was extremely interested in one-day cricket,' Sir Edward recalled. 'He was an academic in a way – and would have got a First at Oxford. But I doubt that his cricket would have been good enough for a Blue or a first class career – I don't think he would have got anywhere. He was made an honorary member of Warwickshire in recognition of the Percy Jeeves link, and he would wear the county tie sometimes, to puzzle Americans. I don't think he was much of a batsman, though he did make some runs at Lord's for the Authors. I asked him once about his innings – and he said: "I would have made a century if the boundaries had been closer."'

Sir Edward feels that once freed of school discipline and its structured game, Wodehouse would have devoted all spare time outside essential study to developing his creative writing. And if it had been a matter of alternatives – either that Oxford acquire a moderate pace bowler for a fleeting couple of seasons, or that the world be blessed by a unique writing talent – then even for those of us captivated by cricket, the choice is clear and unarguable. P.G. Wodehouse will write for our eternal delectation, rather than be just another useful cricketing amateur of the Golden Age.

The MCC Match

On the Monday morning Mike passed the notice-board just as Burgess turned away from pinning up the list of the team to play the MCC. He read it, and his heart missed a beat. For, bottom but one, just above the W.B. Burgess, was a name that leaped from the paper at him. His own name.

If the day happens to be fine, there is a curious, dream-like atmosphere about the opening stages of a first eleven match. Everything seems hushed and expectant. The rest of the school have gone in after the interval at eleven o'clock, and you are alone on the grounds with a cricket-bag. The only signs of life are a few pedestrians on the road beyond the railings and one or two blazer and flannel-clad forms in the pavilion. The sense of isolation is trying to the nerves, and a school team usually bats 25 per cent better after lunch, when the strangeness has worn off.

Mike walked across from Wain's, where he had changed, feeling quite hollow. He could almost have cried with pure fright. Bob had shouted after him from a window as he passed Donaldson's, to wait, so that they could walk over together; but conversation was the last thing Mike desired at that moment.

He had almost reached the pavilion when one of the MCC team came down the steps, saw him, and stopped dead.

'By Jove, Saunders!' cried Mike.

'Why, Master Mike!'

The professional beamed, and quite suddenly, the lost, hopeless feeling left Mike. He felt as cheerful as if he and Saunders had met in the meadow at home, and were just going to begin a little quiet net-practice.

'Why, Master Mike, you don't mean to say you're playing for the school already?'

Mike nodded happily.

'Isn't it ripping,' he said.

Saunders slapped his leg in a sort of ecstasy.

'Didn't I always say it, sir,' he chuckled. 'Wasn't I right? I used to say to myself it 'ud be a pretty good school team that 'ud leave you out.'

'Of course, I'm only playing as a sub., you know. Three chaps are in extra, and I got one of the places.'

'Well, you'll make a hundred today, Master Mike, and then they'll have to put you in.'

'Wish I could!'

'Master Joe's come down with the Club,' said Saunders.

'Joe! Has he really? How ripping! Hullo, here he is. Hullo, Joe?'

The greatest of all the Jacksons was descending the pavilion steps with the gravity befitting an All England batsman. He stopped short, as Saunders had done.

'Mike! You aren't playing!'

'Yes.'

THE MCC MATCH

'Well, I'm hanged! Young marvel, isn't he, Saunders?'

'He is, sir,' said Saunders. 'Got all the strokes. I always said it, Master Joe. Only wants the strength.'

Joe took Mike by the shoulder, and walked him off in the direction of a man in a Zingari blazer who was bowling slows to another of the MCC team. Mike recognised him with awe as one of the three best amateur wicket-keepers in the country.

'What do you think of this?' said Joe, exhibiting Mike, who grinned bashfully. 'Aged ten last birthday, and playing for the school. You *are* only ten, aren't you, Mike?'

'Brother of yours?' asked the wicket-keeper.

'Probably too proud to own the relationship, but he is.'

'This is our star. You wait till he gets at us today. Saunders is our only bowler, and Mike's been brought up on Saunders. You'd better win the toss if you want a chance of getting a knock and lifting your average out of the minuses.'

'I *have* won the toss,' said the other with dignity. 'Do you think I don't know the elementary duties of a captain?'

The school went out to field with mixed feelings. The wicket was hard and true, which would have made it pleasant to be going in first. On the other hand, they would feel decidedly better and fitter for centuries after the game had been in progress an hour or so. Burgess was glad as a private individual, sorry as a captain. For himself, the sooner he got hold of the ball and began to bowl the better he liked it. As a captain, he realised that a side with Joe Jackson on it, not to mention the other first-class men, was not a side to which he would have preferred to give away an advantage. Mike was feeling that by no possibility could he hold the simplest catch, and hoping that nothing would come his way. Bob, conscious of being an uncertain field, was feeling just the same.

The MCC opened with Joe and a man in an Oxford Authentic cap. The beginning of the game was quiet. Burgess's yorker was nearly too much for the latter in the first over, but he contrived to chop it away, and the pair gradually settled down. At twenty, Joe began to open his shoulders. Twenty became forty with disturbing swiftness, and Burgess tried a change of bowling.

It seemed for one instant as if the move had been a success, for Joe, still taking risks, tried to late-cut a rising ball, and snicked it straight into Bob's hands at second slip. It was the easiest of slip-catches, but Bob fumbled it, dropped it, almost held it a second time, and finally let it fall miserably to the ground. It was a moment too painful for words. He rolled the ball back to the bowler in silence.

One of those weary periods followed when the batsman's defence seems to the fieldsmen absolutely impregnable. There was a sickening inevitableness in the way in which every ball was played with the very centre of the bat. And, as usual, just when things seemed most hopeless, relief came. The Authentic, getting in front of his wicket, to pull one of the simplest long-hops ever seen on a cricket field, missed it, and was lbw. And the next ball upset the newcomer's leg stump.

The school revived. Bowlers and field were infused with a new life. Another wicket – two stumps knocked out of the ground by Burgess – helped the thing on. When the bell rang for the end of morning school, five wickets were down for a hundred and thirteen.

But from the end of school till lunch things went very wrong indeed. Joe was still in at one end, invincible; and at the other was the great wicket-keeper. And the pair of them suddenly began to force the pace till the bowling was in a tangled knot. Four after four, all round the wicket, with never a chance or a mishit to vary the monotony. Two hundred went up, and two hundred and fifty. Then Joe reached his century, and was stumped next ball. Then came lunch.

The rest of the innings was like the gentle rain after the thunderstorm. Runs came with fair regularity, but wickets fell at intervals, and when the wicket-keeper was run out at length for a lively sixty-three, the end was very near. Saunders, coming in last, hit two boundaries, and was then caught by Mike. His second hit had just lifted the MCC total over the three hundred.

Three hundred is a score that takes some making on any ground, but on a fine day it was not an unusual total for the Wrykyn eleven. Some years before, against Ripton, they had run up four hundred and sixteen; and only last season had massacred a very weak team of Old Wrykynians with a score that only just missed the fourth hundred.

Unfortunately, on the present occasion, there was scarcely time, unless the bowling happened to get completely collared, to make the runs. It was a quarter to four when the innings began, and stumps were to be drawn at a quarter to seven. A hundred an hour is quick work.

Burgess, however, was optimistic, as usual. 'Better have a go for them,' he said to Berridge and Marsh, the school first pair.

Following out this courageous advice, Berridge, after hitting three boundaries in his first two overs, was stumped half-way through the third.

After this, things settled down. Morris, the first-wicket man, was a thoroughly sound bat, a little on the slow side, but exceedingly hard to shift. He and Marsh proceeded to play themselves in, until it looked as if they were likely to stay till the drawing of stumps.

A comfortable, rather somnolent feeling settled upon the school. A long stand at cricket is a soothing sight to watch. There was an absence of hurry about the batsmen which harmonised well with the drowsy summer afternoon. And yet runs were coming at a fair pace. The hundred went up at five o'clock, the hundred and fifty at half-past. Both batsmen were completely at home, and the MCC third-change bowlers had been put on.

Then the great wicket-keeper took off the pads and gloves, and the fieldsmen retired to posts at the extreme edge of the ground.

'Lobs,' said Burgess. 'By Jove, I wish I was in.'

It seemed to be the general opinion among the members of the Wrykyn eleven on the pavilion balcony that Morris and Marsh were in luck. The team did not grudge them their good fortune, because they had earned it; but they were distinctly envious.

Lobs are the most dangerous, insinuating things in the world. Everybody knows in theory the right way to treat them. Everybody knows that the man who is content not to try to score more than a single cannot get out to them. Yet nearly everybody does get out to them.

It was the same story today. The first over yielded six runs, all through gentle taps along the ground. In the second, Marsh hit an over-pitched one along the ground to the terrace bank. The next ball he swept round to the leg boundary. And that was the end of Marsh. He saw himself scoring at the rate of twenty-four an over. Off the last ball he was stumped by several feet, having done himself credit by scoring seventy.

The long stand was followed, as usual, by a series of disasters. Marsh's wicket had fallen at a hundred and eighty. Ellerby left at a hundred and eighty-six. By the time the scoring-board registered two hundred, five wickets were down, three of them victims to the lobs. Morris was still in at one end. He had refused to be tempted. He was jogging on steadily to his century.

Bob Jackson went in next, with instructions to keep his eye on the lob-man.

For a time things went well. Saunders, who had gone on to bowl again after a rest, seemed to give Morris no trouble, and Bob put him through the slips with apparent ease. Twenty runs were added, when the lob-bowler once more got in his deadly work. Bob, letting alone a ball wide of the off-stump under the impression that it was going to break away, was disagreeably surprised to find it break in instead, and hit the wicket. The bowler smiled sadly, as if he hated to have to do these things.

Mike's heart jumped as he saw the bails go. It was his turn next.

'Two hundred and twenty-nine,' said Burgess, 'and it's ten past six. No good trying for the runs now. Stick in,' he added to Mike. 'That's all you've got to do.'

All! . . . Mike felt as if he was being strangled. His heart was racing like the engines of a motor. He knew his teeth were chattering. He wished he could stop them. What a time Bob was taking to get back to the pavilion! He wanted to rush out, and get the thing over.

At last he arrived, and Mike, fumbling at a glove, tottered out into the sunshine. He heard miles and miles away a sound of clapping, and a thin, shrill noise as if somebody were screaming in the distance. As a matter of fact, several members of his form and of the junior day-room at Wain's nearly burst themselves at that moment.

At the wickets, he felt better. Bob had fallen to the last ball of the over, and Morris, standing ready for Saunders's delivery, looked so calm and certain of himself that it was impossible to feel entirely without hope and self-confidence. Mike knew that Morris had made ninety-eight, and he supposed that Morris knew that he was very near his century; yet he seemed to be absolutely undisturbed. Mike drew courage from his attitude.

Morris pushed the first ball away to leg.

Mike would have liked to have run two, but short leg had retrieved the ball as he reached the crease.

The moment had come, the moment which he had experienced only in dreams. And in the dreams he was always full of confidence, and invariably hit a boundary. Sometimes a drive, sometimes a cut, but always a boundary.

'To leg, sir,' said the umpire.

'Don't be in a funk,' said a voice. 'Play straight, and you can't get out.'

It was Joe, who had taken the gloves when the wicket-keeper went on to bowl.

Mike grinned, wryly but gratefully.

Saunders was beginning his run. It was all so home-like that for a moment Mike felt himself again. How often he had seen those two little skips and the jump. It was like being in the paddock again, with Marjory and the dogs waiting by the railings to fetch the ball if he made a drive.

Saunders ran to the crease, and bowled.

Now, Saunders was a conscientious man, and, doubtless, bowled the very best ball that he possibly could. On the other hand, it was Mike's first appearance for the school, and Saunders, besides being conscientious, was undoubtedly kind-hearted. It is useless to speculate as to whether he was trying to bowl his best that ball. If so, he failed signally. It was a half-volley, just the right distance away from the off-stump; the sort of ball Mike was wont to send nearly through the net at home. . . .

The next moment the dreams had come true. The umpire was signalling to the scoring-box, the school was shouting, extra-cover was trotting to the boundary to fetch the ball, and Mike was blushing and wondering whether it was bad form to grin.

From that ball onwards all was for the best in this best of all possible worlds. Saunders bowled no more half-volleys; but Mike played everything that he did bowl. He met the lobs with a bat like a barn-door. Even the departure of Morris, caught in the slips off Saunders's next over for a chanceless hundred and five, did not disturb him. All nervousness had left him. He felt equal to the situation. Burgess came in, and began to hit out as if he meant to knock off the runs. The bowling became a shade loose. Twice he was given half tosses to leg, which he hit to the terrace bank. Half-past six chimed, and two hundred and fifty went up on the telegraph board. Burgess continued to hit. Mike's whole soul was concentrated on keeping up his wicket. There was only Reeves to follow him, and Reeves was a victim to the first straight ball. Burgess had to hit because it was the only game he knew; but he himself must simply stay in.

The hands of the clock seemed to have stopped. Then suddenly he heard the umpire say 'Last over,' and he settled down to keep those six balls out of his wicket.

The lob bowler had taken himself off, and the Oxford Authentic had gone on, fast left-hand.

The first ball was short and wide of the off-stump. Mike let it alone. Number two: yorker. Got him! Three: straight half-volley. Mike played it back to the bowler. Four: beat him, and missed the wicket by an inch. Five: another yorker. Down on it again in the old familiar way.

All was well. The match was a draw now whatever happened to him. He hit out, almost at a venture, at the last ball, and mid-off, jumping, just failed to reach it. It hummed over his head, and ran like a streak along the turf and up the bank, and a great howl of delight went up from the school as the umpire took off the bails.

Mike walked away from the wickets with Joe and the wicket-keeper.

'I'm sorry about your nose, Joe,' said the wicket-keeper in tones of grave solicitude.

'What's wrong with it?'

'At present,' said the wicket-keeper, 'nothing. But in a few years I'm afraid it's going to be put badly out of joint.'

The Match with Downing's

It is a curious instinct which prompts most people to rub a thing in that makes the lot of the average convert an unhappy one. Only the very self-controlled can refrain from improving the occasion and scoring off the convert. Most leap at the opportunity.

It was so in Mike's case. Mike was not a genuine convert, but to Mr Downing he had the outward aspect of one. When you have been impressing upon a non-cricketing boy for nearly a month that (*a*) the school is above all a keen school, (*b*) that all members of it should play cricket, and (*c*) that by not playing cricket he is ruining his chances in this world and imperilling them in the next; and when, quite unexpectedly, you come upon this boy dressed in cricket flannels, wearing cricket boots and carrying a cricket bag, it seems only natural to assume that you have converted him, that the seeds of your eloquence have fallen on fruitful soil and sprouted.

Mr Downing assumed it.

He was walking to the field with Adair and another member of his team when he came upon Mike.

'What!' he cried. 'Our Jackson clad in a suit of mail and armed for the fray!'

This was Mr Downing's No.2 manner – the playful.

'This is indeed Saul among the prophets. Why this sudden enthusiasm for a game which I understood that you despised? Are our opponents so reduced?'

Psmith, who was with Mike, took charge of the affair with a languid grace which had maddened hundreds in its time, and which never failed to ruffle Mr Downing.

'We are, above all, sir,' he said, 'a keen house. Drones are not welcomed by us. We are essentially versatile. Jackson, the archaeologist of yesterday becomes the cricketer of today. It is the right spirit, sir,' said Psmith earnestly. 'I like to see it.'

'Indeed, Smith? You are not playing yourself, I notice. Your enthusiasm has bounds.'

'In our house, sir, competition is fierce, and the Selection Committee unfortunately passed me over.'

There were a number of pitches dotted about over the field, for there was always a touch of the London Park about it on Midterm Service day. Adair, as captain of cricket, had naturally selected the best for his own match. It was a good wicket, Mike saw. As a matter of fact the wickets at Sedleigh were nearly always good. Adair had infected the ground-man with some of his own keenness, with the result that that once-leisurely official now found himself sometimes, with a kind of mild surprise, working really hard. At the beginning of the previous season Sedleigh had played a scratch team from a neighbouring town on a wicket which, except for the creases, was absolutely undistinguishable from the surrounding turf, and behind the pavilion after the match Adair had spoken certain home truths to the ground-man. The latter's reformation had dated from that moment.

Barnes, timidly jubilant, came up to Mike with the news that he had won the toss, and the request that Mike would go in first with him.

In stories of the 'Not Really a Duffer' type, where the nervous new boy, who has been found crying in the changing-room over the photograph of his sister, contrives to get an innings in a game, nobody suspects that he is really a prodigy till he hits the Bully's first ball out of the ground for six.

With Mike it was different. There was no pitying smile on Adair's face as he started his run preparatory to sending down the first ball. Mike, on the cricket field, could not have looked anything but a cricketer if he had turned out in a tweed suit and hobnail boots. Cricketer was written all over him – in his walk, in the way he took guard, in his stand at the wickets. Adair started to bowl with the feeling that this was somebody who had more than a little knowledge of how to deal with good bowling and punish bad.

Mike started cautiously. He was more than usually anxious to make runs today, and he meant to take no risks till he could afford to do so. He had seen Adair bowl at the nets, and he knew that he was good.

The first over was a maiden, six dangerous balls beautifully played. The fieldsmen changed over.

The general interest had now settled on the

match between Outwood's and Downing's. The fact in Mike's case had gone round the field, and, as several of the other games had not yet begun, quite a large crowd had collected near the pavilion to watch. Mike's masterly treatment of the opening over had impressed the spectators, and there was a popular desire to see how he would deal with Mr Downing's slows. It was generally anticipated that he would do something special with them.

Off the first ball of the master's over a leg-bye was run.

Mike took guard.

Mr Downing was a bowler with a style of his own. He took two short steps, two long steps, gave a jump, took three more short steps, and ended with a combination of step and jump, during which the ball emerged from behind his back and started on its slow career to the wicket. The whole business had some of the dignity of the old-fashioned minuet, subtly blended with the careless vigour of a cake-walk. The ball, when delivered, was billed to break from leg, but the programme was subject to alterations.

If the spectators had expected Mike to begin any firework effects with the first ball, they were disappointed. He played the over through with a grace worthy of his brother Joe. The last ball he turned to leg for a single.

His treatment of Adair's next over was freer. He had got a sight of the ball now. Halfway through the over a beautiful square cut forced a passage through the crowd by the pavilion, and dashed up against the rails. He drove the sixth ball past cover for three.

The crowd was now reluctantly dispersing to its own games, but it stopped as Mr Downing started his minuet-cake-walk, in the hope that it might see something more sensational.

This time the hope was fulfilled.

The ball was well up, slow, and off the wicket on the on-side. Perhaps if it had been allowed to pitch, it might have broken in and become quite dangerous. Mike went out at it, and hit it a couple of feet from the ground. The ball dropped with a thud and a spurting of dust in the road that ran along one side of the cricket field.

It was returned on the instalment system by helpers from other games, and the bowler began his manoeuvres again. A half-volley this time. Mike slammed it back, and mid-on, whose heart was obviously not in the thing, failed to stop it.

'Get to them, Jenkins,' said Mr Downing irritably, as the ball came back from the boundary. 'Get to them.'

'Sir, please, sir –'

'Don't talk in the field, Jenkins.'

Having had a full-pitch hit for six and a half-volley for four, there was a strong probability that Mr Downing would pitch his next ball short.

The expected happened. The third ball was a slow long-hop and hit the road at about the same spot where the first had landed. A howl of untuneful applause rose from the watchers in the pavilion, and Mike, with the feeling that this sort of bowling was too good to be true, waited in position for number four.

There are moments when a sort of panic

seizes a bowler. This happened now with Mr Downing. He suddenly abandoned science and ran amok. His run lost its stateliness and increased its vigour. He charged up to the wicket as a wounded buffalo sometimes charges a gun. His whole idea now was to bowl fast.

When a slow bowler starts to bowl fast, it is usually as well to be batting, if you can manage it.

By the time the over was finished, Mike's score had been increased by sixteen, and the total of his side, in addition, by three wides.

And a shrill small voice, from the neighbourhood of the pavilion, uttered with painful distinctness the words, 'Take him off!'

That was how the most sensational day's cricket began that Sedleigh had known.

A description of the details of the morning's play would be monotonous. It is enough to say that they ran on much the same lines as the third and fourth overs of the match. Mr Downing bowled one more over, off which Mike helped himself to sixteen runs, and then retired moodily to cover-point, where, in Adair's fifth over, he missed Barnes – the first occasion since the game began on which that mild batsman had attempted to score more than a single. Scared by this escape, Outwood's captain shrank back into his shell, sat on the splice like a limpet, and, offering no more chances, was not out at lunch time with a score of eleven.

Mike had then made a hundred and three.

As Mike was taking off his pads in the pavilion, Adair came up.

'Why did you say you didn't play cricket?' he asked abruptly.

When one has been bowling the whole morning, and bowling well, without the slightest success, one is inclined to be abrupt.

Mike finished unfastening an obstinate strap. Then he looked up.

'I didn't say anything of the kind. I said I wasn't going to play here. There's a difference. As a matter of fact, I was in the Wrykyn team before I came here. Three years.'

Adair was silent for a moment.

'Will you play for us against the Old Sedleighans tomorrow?' he said at length.

Mike tossed his pads into his bag and got up.

'No, thanks.'

There was a silence.

'Above it, I suppose?'

'Not a bit. Not up to it. I shall want a lot of coaching at that end net of yours before I'm fit to play for Sedleigh.'

There was another pause.

'Then you won't play?' asked Adair.

'I'm not keeping you, am I?' said Mike, politely.

It was remarkable what a number of members of Outwood's house appeared to cherish a personal grudge against Mr Downing. It had been that master's somewhat injudicious practice for many years to treat his own house as a sort of Chosen People. Of all masters, the most unpopular is he who by the silent tribunal of a school is convicted of favouritism. And the dislike deepens if it is a house which he favours and not merely individuals. On occasions when boys in his own house and boys from other houses were accomplices and partners in wrong-doing, Mr Downing distributed his thunderbolts unequally, and the school noticed it. The result was that not only he himself, but also – which was rather unfair – his house, too, had acquired a good deal of unpopularity.

The general consensus of opinion in Outwood's during the luncheon interval was that having got Downing's up a tree, they would be fools not to make the most of the situation.

Barnes's remark that he supposed, unless anything happened and wickets began to fall a bit faster, they had better think of declaring somewhere about half-past three or four, was met with a storm of opposition.

'Declare!' said Robinson. 'Great Scott, what on earth are you talking about?'

'Declare!' Stone's voice was almost a wail of indignation. 'I never saw such a chump.'

'They'll be rather sick if we don't, won't they?' suggested Barnes.

'Sick! I should think they would,' said Stone. 'That's just the gay idea. Can't you see that by a miracle we've got a chance of getting a jolly good bit of our own back against those Downing's ticks? What we've got to do is to jolly well keep them in the field all day if we can, and be jolly glad it's so beastly hot. If they lose about a dozen pounds each through sweating about in the sun after Jackson's drives, perhaps they'll stick on less side about things in general in future. Besides, I want an innings against that bilge of old Downing's, if I can get it.'

'So do I,' said Robinson.

'If you declare, I swear I won't field. Nor will Robinson.'

'Rather not.'

'Well, I won't then,' said Barnes unhappily. 'Only you know they're rather sick already.'

'Don't you worry about that,' said Stone with a wide grin. 'They'll be a lot sicker before we've finished.'

And so it came about that that particular Mid-term Service day match made history. Big scores had often been put up on Mid-term Service day. Games had frequently been one-sided. But it had never happened before in the annals of the school that one side, going in early in the morning, had neither completed its innings nor declared it closed when stumps were drawn at 6.30. In no previous Sedleigh match, after a full day's play, had the pathetic words 'Did not bat' been written against the whole of one of the contending teams.

These are the things which mark epochs.

Play was resumed at 2.15. For a quarter of an hour Mike was comparatively quiet. Adair, fortified by food and rest, was bowling really well, and his first half-dozen overs had to be watched carefully. But the wicket was too good to give him a chance, and Mike, playing hiself in again, proceeded to get to business once more. Bowlers came and went. Adair pounded away at one end with brief intervals between the attacks. Mr. Downing took a couple more overs, in one of which a horse, passing in the road, nearly had its useful life cut suddenly short. Change-bowlers of various actions and paces, each weirder and more futile than the last, tried their luck. But still the first-wicket stand continued.

The bowling of a house team is all head

and no body. The first pair probably have some idea of length and break. The first-change pair are poor. And the rest, the small-change, are simply the sort of things one sees in dreams after a heavy supper, or when one is out without one's gun.

Time, mercifully, generally breaks up a big stand at cricket before the field has suffered too much, and that is what happened now. At four o'clock, when the score stood at two hundred and twenty for no wicket, Barnes, greatly daring, smote lustily at a rather wide half-volley and was caught at short-slip for thirty-three. He retired blushfully to the pavilion, amidst applause, and Stone came out.

As Mike had then made a hundred and eighty-seven, it was assumed by the field, that directly he had topped his second century, the closure would be applied and their ordeal finished. There was almost a sigh of relief when frantic cheering from the crowd told that the feat had been accomplished. The fieldsmen clapped in quite an indulgent sort of way, as who should say, 'Capital, capital. And now let's start *our* innings.' Some even began to edge towards the pavilion.

But the next ball was bowled, and the next over, and the next after that, and still Barnes made no sign. (The conscience-stricken captain of Outwood's was, as a matter of fact, being practically held down by Robinson and other ruffians by force.)

A grey dismay settled on the field.

The bowling had now become almost unbelievably bad. Lobs were being tried, and Stone, nearly weeping with pure joy, was playing an innings of the How-to-brighten-cricket type. He had an unorthodox style, but an excellent eye, and the road at this period of the game became absolutely unsafe for pedestrians and traffic.

Mike's pace had become slower, as was only natural, but his score, too, was mounting steadily.

'This is foolery,' snapped Mr Downing, as the three hundred and fifty went up on the board. 'Barnes!' he called.

There was no reply. A committee of three was at that moment engaged in sitting on Barnes's head in the first eleven changing-room, in order to correct a more than usually feverish attack of conscience.

'Barnes!'

'Please, sir.' said Stone, some species of telepathy telling him what was detaining his captain. 'I think Barnes must have left the field. He has probably gone over to the house to fetch something.'

'This is absurd. You must declare your innings closed. The game has become a farce.'

'Declare! Sir, we can't unless Barnes does. He might be awfully annoyed if we did anything like that without consulting him.'

'Absurd.'

'He's very touchy sir.'

'It is perfect foolery.'

'I think Jenkins is just going to bowl, sir.'

Mr Downing walked moodily to his place.

In a neat wooden frame in the senior day-room at Outwood's, just above the mantel-piece, there was on view, a week later, a slip of paper.

The writing on it was as follows:

OUTWOOD'S *v.* DOWNING'S
Outwood's. First innings

J.P. Barnes, *c.* Hammond, *b.* Hassall	33
M. Jackson, not out	277
W.J. Stone, not out	124
Extras	37
Total (for one wicket)	471

Downing's did not bat.

At Lord's

Mike got to Lord's just as the umpires moved out into the field. He raced round to the pavilion. Joe met him on the stairs.

'It's all right,' he said. 'No hurry. We've won the toss. I've put you in fourth wicket.'

'Right ho,' said Mike. 'Glad we haven't to field just yet.'

'We oughtn't to have to field today if we don't chuck our wickets away.'

'Good wicket?'

'Like a billiard-table. I'm glad you were able to come. Have any difficulty in getting away?'

Joe Jackson's knowledge of the workings of a bank was of the slightest. He himself had never, since he left Oxford, been in a position where there were obstacles to getting off to play in first-class cricket. By profession he was agent to a sporting baronet whose hobby was the cricket of the county, and so, far from finding any difficulty in playing for the county, he was given to understand by his employer that that was his chief duty. It never occurred to him that Mike might find his bank less amenable in the matter of giving leave. His only fear, when he rang Mike up that morning, had been that this might be a particularly busy day at the New Asiatic Bank. If there was no special rush of work, he took it for granted that Mike would simply go to the manager, ask for leave to play in the match, and be given it with a beaming smile.

Mike did not answer the question, but asked one on his own account.

'How did you happen to be short?' he said.

'It was rotten luck. It was like this. We were altering our team after the Sussex match, to bring in Ballard, Keene, and Willis. They couldn't get down to Brighton, as the 'Varsity had a match, but there was nothing on for them in the last half of the week, so they'd promised to roll up.'

Ballard, Keene, and Willis were members of the Cambridge team, all very capable performers and much in demand by the county, when they could get away to play for it.

'Well?' said Mike.

'Well, we all came up by train from Brighton last night. But these three asses had arranged to motor down from Cambridge early today, and get here in time for the start. What happens? Why, Willis, who fancies himself as a chauffeur, undertakes to do the driving; and naturally, being an absolute rotter, goes and smashes up the whole concern just outside St Albans. The first thing I knew of it was when I got to Lord's at half-past ten, and found a wire waiting for me to say that they were all three of them crocked, and couldn't possibly play. I tell you, it was a bit of a jar to get half an hour before the match started. Willis has sprained his ankle, apparently; Keene's damaged his wrist; and Ballard has smashed his collar-bone. I don't suppose they'll be able to play in the 'Varsity match. Rotten luck for Cambridge. Well, fortunately we'd had two reserve pros with us at Brighton, who had come up to London with the team in case they might be wanted, so, with them, we were only one short. Then I thought of you. That's how it was.'

'I see,' said Mike. 'Who are the pros?'

'Davis and Brockley. Both bowlers. It weakens our batting a lot. Ballard or Willis might have got a stack of runs on this wicket. Still, we've got a certain amount of batting as it is. We oughtn't to do badly, if we're careful. You've been getting some practice, I suppose, this season?'

'In a sort of a way. Nets and so on. No matches of any importance.'

'Dash it, I wish you'd had a game or two in decent class cricket. Still, nets are better than nothing, I hope you'll be in form. We may want a pretty long knock from you, if things go wrong. These men seem to be settling down all right, thank goodness,' he added, looking out of the window at the county's first pair, Warrington and Mills, two professionals, who, as the result of ten minutes' play, had put up twenty.

'I'd better go and change,' said Mike, picking up his bag. 'You're in first wicket, I suppose?'

'Yes. And Reggie, second wicket.'

Reggie was another of Mike's brothers, not nearly so fine a player as Joe, but a sound bat, who generally made runs if allowed to stay in.

Mike changed, and went out into the little balcony at the top of the pavilion. He had it to himself. There were not many spectators in the pavilion at this early stage of the game.

There are few more restful places, if one wishes to think, than the upper balconies of Lord's pavilion. Mike, watching the game making its leisurely progress on the turf below, set himself seriously to review the situation in all its aspects. The exhilaration of bursting the bonds had begun to fade, and he found himself able to look into the matter of his desertion and weigh up the consequences. There was no doubt that he had cut the painter once and for all. Even a friendly-disposed management could hardly overlook what he had done. And the management of the New Asiatic Bank was the very reverse of friendly. Mr Bickersdyke, he knew, would jump at this chance of getting rid of him. He realised that he must look on his career in the bank as a closed book. It was definitely over, and he must now think about the future.

It was not a time for half-measures. He could not go home. He must carry the thing through, now that he had begun, and find something definite to do, to support himself.

There seemed only one opening for him. What could he do, he asked himself. Just one thing. He could play cricket. It was by his cricket that he must live. He would have to become a professional. Could he get taken on? That was the question. It was impossible that he should play for his own county on his residential qualification. He could not appear as a professional in the same team in which his brothers were playing as amateurs. He must stake all on his birth qualification for Surrey.

On the other hand, had he the credentials

which Surrey would want? He had a school reputation. But was that enough? He could not help feeling that it might not be.

Thinking it over more tensely than he had ever thought over anything in his whole life, he saw clearly that everything depended on what sort of a show he made in this match which was now in progress. It was his big chance. If he succeeded, all would be well. He did not care to think what his position would be if he did not succeed.

A distant appeal and a sound of clapping from the crowd broke in on his thoughts. Mills was out, caught at the wicket. The telegraph-board gave the total as forty-eight. Not sensational. The success of the team depended largely on what sort of a start the two professionals made.

The clapping broke out again as Joe made his way down the steps. Joe, as an All England player, was a favourite with the crowd.

Mike watched him play an over in his strong, graceful style: then it suddenly occurred to him that he would like to know how matters had gone at the bank in his absence.

He went down to the telephone, rang up the bank, and asked for Psmith.

Presently the familiar voice made itself heard.

'Hullo, Smith.'

'Hullo. Is that Comrade Jackson? How are things progressing?'

'Fairly well. We're in first. We've lost one wicket, and the fifty's just up. I say, what's happened at the bank?'

'I broke the news to Comrade Gregory. A

charming personality. I feel that we shall be friends.'

'Was he sick?'

'In a measure, yes. Indeed, I may say he practically foamed at the mouth. I explained the situation, but he was not to be appeased. He jerked me into the presence of Comrade Bickersdyke, with whom I had a brief but entertaining chat. He had not a great deal to say, but he listened attentively to my narrative, and eventually told me off to take your place in the Fixed Deposits. That melancholy task I am now performing to the best of my ability. I find the work a little trying. There is too much ledger-lugging to be done for my simple tastes. I have been hauling ledgers from the safe all the morning. The cry is beginning to go round, "Psmith is willing, but can his physique stand the strain?" In the excitement of the moment just now I dropped a some-what massive tome onto Comrade Gregory's foot, unfortunately, I understand, the foot in which he has of late been suffering twinges of gout. I passed the thing off with ready tact, but I cannot deny that there was a certain tempo-rary coolness, which, indeed, is not yet past. These things, Comrade Jackson, are the whirlpools in the quiet stream of commercial life.'

'Have I got the sack?'

'No official pronouncement has been made to me as yet on the subject, but I think I should advise you, if you are offered another job in the course of the day, to accept it. I can-not say that you are precisely the pet of the management just at present. However, I have ideas for your future, which I will divulge when we meet. I propose to slide coyly from the office at about four o'clock. I am meeting my father at that hour. We shall come straight on to Lord's.'

'Right ho,' said Mike. 'I'll be looking out for you.'

'Is there any little message I can give Comrade Gregory from you?'

'You can give him my love, if you like.'

'It shall be done. Good-bye.'

'Good-bye.'

Mike replaced the receiver, and went up to his balcony again.

As soon as his eye fell on the telegraph-board he saw with a start that things had been moving rapidly in his brief absence. The numbers of the batsmen on the board were three and five.

'Great Scott!' he cried. 'Why, I'm in next. What on earth's been happening?'

He put on his pads hurriedly, expecting every moment that a wicket would fall and find him unprepared. But the batsmen were still together when he rose, ready for the fray, and went downstairs to get news.

He found his brother Reggie in the dressing-room.

'What's happened?' he said. 'How were you out?'

'LBW,' said Reggie. 'Goodness knows how it happened. My eyesight must be going. I mistimed the thing altogether.'

'How was Warrington out?'

'Caught in the slips.'

'By Jove!' said Mike. 'This is pretty rocky. Three for sixty-one. We shall get mopped.'

'Unless you and Joe do something. There's

no earthly need to get out. The wicket's as good as you want, and the bowling's nothing special. Well played, Joe!'

A beautiful glide to leg by the greatest of the Jacksons had rolled up against the pavilion rails. The fieldsmen changed across for the next over.

'If only Peters stops a bit –' began Mike, and broke off. Peters' off stump was lying at an angle of forty-five degrees.

'Well, he hasn't,' said Reggie grimly. 'Silly ass, why did he hit at that one? All he'd got to do was to stay in with Joe. Now it's up to you. Do try and do something, or we'll be out under the hundred.'

Mike waited till the outcoming batsman had turned in at the professionals' gate. Then he walked down the steps and out into the open, feeling more nervous than he had felt since that far-off day when he had first gone in to bat for Wrykyn against the MCC. He found his thoughts flying back to that occasion. Today, as then, everything seemed very distant and unreal. The spectators were miles away. He had often been to Lord's as a spectator, but the place seemed entirely unfamiliar now. He felt as if he were in a strange land.

He was conscious of Joe leaving the crease to meet him on his way. He smiled feebly. 'Buck up,' said Joe in that robust way of his which was so heartening. 'Nothing in the bowling, and the wicket like a shirt-front. Play just as if you were at the nets. And for goodness' sake don't try to score all your runs in the first over. Stick in, and we've got them.'

Mike smiled again more feebly than

before, and made a weird gurgling noise in his throat.

It had been the Middlesex fast bowler who had destroyed Peters. Mike was not sorry. He did not object to fast bowling. He took guard, and looked round him, taking careful note of the positions of the slips.

As usual, once he was at the wicket the paralysed feeling left him. He became conscious again of his power. Dash it all, what was there to be afraid of? He was a jolly good bat, and he would jolly well show them that he was, too.

The fast bowler, with a preliminary bound, began his run. Mike settled himself into position, his whole soul concentrated on the ball. Everything else was wiped from his mind.

For nearly two hours Mike had been experiencing the keenest pleasure that it had ever fallen to his lot to feel. From the moment he took his first ball till the luncheon interval he had suffered the acutest discomfort. His nervousness had left him to a great extent, but he had never really settled down. Sometimes by luck, and sometimes by skill, he had kept the ball out of his wicket; but he was scratching, and he knew it. Not for a single over had he been comfortable. On several occasions he had edged balls to leg and through the slips in quite an inferior manner, and it was seldom that he managed to hit with the centre of the bat.

Nobody is more alive to the fact that he is not playing up to his true form than the batsman. Even though his score mounted little by little into the twenties, Mike was miserable. If this was the best he could do on a perfect wicket, he felt there was not much hope for him as a professional.

The poorness of his play was accentuated by the brilliance of Joe's. Joe combined science and vigour to a remarkable degree. He laid on the wood with a graceful robustness which drew much cheering from the crowd. Beside him Mike was oppressed by that leaden sense of moral inferiority which weighs on a man who has turned up to dinner in ordinary clothes when everybody else has dressed. He felt awkward and conspicuously out of place.

Then came lunch – and after lunch a glorious change.

Volumes might be written on the cricket lunch and the influence it has on the run of the game; how it undoes one man, and sends another back to the fray like a giant refreshed; how it turns the brilliant fast bowler into the sluggish medium, and the nervous bat into the masterful smiter.

On Mike its effect was magical. He lunched wisely and well, chewing his food with the concentration of a thirty-three bites a mouthful crank, and drinking dry ginger-ale. As he walked out with Joe after the interval he knew that a change had taken place in him. His nerve had come back, and with it his form.

It sometimes happens at cricket that when one feels particularly fit one gets snapped in the slips in the first over, or clean bowled by a full toss; but neither of these things happened to Mike. He stayed in, and began to score. Now there were no edgings through the slips and snicks to leg. He was meeting the ball in the centre of the bat, and meeting it vigorously. Two boundaries in successive balls off the fast bowler, hard, clean drives past extra-cover, put him at peace with all the world. He was on top. He had found himself.

Joe, at the other end, resumed his brilliant career. His century and Mike's fifty arrived in the same over. The bowling began to grow loose.

Joe, having reached his century, slowed down somewhat, and Mike took up the running. The score rose rapidly.

A leg-theory bowler kept down the pace of the run-getting for a time, but the bowlers at the other end continued to give away runs. Mike's score passed from sixty to seventy, from seventy to eighty, from eighty to ninety. When the Smiths, father and son, came on to the ground the total was ninety-eight. Joe had made a hundred and thirty-three.

Mike reached his century just as Psmith and his father took their seats. A square cut off the slow bowler was just too wide for point to get to. By the time third man had sprinted across and returned the ball the batsmen had run two.

Mr Smith was enthusiastic.

'I tell you,' he said to Psmith, who was clapping in a gently encouraging manner, 'the boy's a wonderful bat. I said so when he was down with us. I remember telling him so myself. "I've seen your brothers play," I said, "and you're better than any of them." I remember it distinctly. He'll be playing for England in another year or two. Fancy putting a cricketer like that into the City! It's a crime.'

'I gather,' said Psmith, 'that the family

coffers had got a bit low. It was necessary for Comrade Jackson to do something by way of saving the Old Home.'

'He ought to be at the University. Look, he's got that man away to the boundary again. They'll never get him out.'

At six o'clock the partnership was broken. Joe running himself out in trying to snatch a single where no single was. He had made a hundred and eighty-nine.

Mike flung himself down on the turf with mixed feelings. He was sorry Joe was out, but he was very glad indeed of the chance of a rest. He was utterly fagged. A half-day match once a week is no training for first-class cricket. Joe, who had been playing all the season, was as tough as india-rubber, and trotted into the pavilion as fresh as if he had been having a brief spell at the nets. Mike, on the other hand, felt that he simply wanted to be dropped into a cold bath and left there indefinitely. There was only another half-hour's play, but he doubted if he could get through it.

He dragged himself up wearily as Joe's successor arrived at the wickets. He had crossed Joe before the latter's downfall, and it was his turn to take the bowling.

Something seemed to have gone out of him. He could not time the ball properly. The last ball of the over looked like a half-volley, and he hit out at it. But it was just short of a half-volley, and his stroke arrived too soon. The bowler, running in the direction of mid-on, brought off an easy c.-and-b.

Mike turned away towards the pavilion. He heard the gradually swelling applause in a sort of dream. It seemed to him hours before he reached the dressing-room.

He was sitting on a chair, wishing that somebody would come along and take off his pads, when Psmith's card was brought to him. A few moments later the old Etonian appeared in person.

'Hullo, Smith,' said Mike, 'By Jove! I'm done.'

'"How Little Willie Saved the Match,"' said Psmith. 'What you want is one of those gin and ginger-beers we hear so much about. Remove those pads, and let us flit downstairs in search of a couple. Well, Comrade Jackson, you have fought the good fight this day. My father sends his compliments. He is dining out, or he would have come up. He is going to look in at the flat latish.'

'How many did I get?' asked Mike. 'I was so jolly done I didn't think of looking.'

'A hundred and forty-eight of the best,' said Psmith. 'What will they say at the old homestead about this? Are you ready? Then let us test this fruity old ginger-beer of theirs.'

The two batsmen who had followed the big stand were apparently having a little stand all of their own. No more wickets fell before the drawing of stumps. Psmith waited for Mike while he changed, and carried him off in a cab to Simpson's, a restaurant which, as he justly observed, offered two great advantages, namely, that you need not dress, and, secondly, that you paid your half-crown, and were then at liberty to eat till you were helpless, if you felt so disposed, without extra charge.

Bingley Crocker
Learns Cricket

Poets have dealt feelingly with the emotions of
practically every variety except one. They
have sung of Ruth, of Israel in bondage, of
slaves pining for their native Africa, and of the
miner's dream of home. But the sorrows of the
baseball enthusiast, compelled by fate to live
three thousand miles away from the Polo
Grounds, have been neglected in song.
Bingley Crocker was such a one, and in summer his agonies were awful. He pined away in
a country where they said 'Well played, sir!'
when they meant 'At-a-boy!'

'Bayliss, do you play cricket?'

'I am a little past the age, sir. In my
younger days –'

'Do you understand it?'

'Yes, sir. I frequently spend an afternoon at
Lord's or the Oval when there is a good
match.'

Many who enjoyed a merely casual
acquaintance with the butler would have
looked on this as an astonishingly unexpected
revelation of humanity in Bayliss, but Mr
Crocker was not surprised. To him, from the
very beginning, Bayliss had been a man and a
brother, who was always willing to suspend
his duties in order to answer questions dealing

89

with the thousand and one problems which the social life of England presented. Mr Crocker's mind had adjusted itself with difficulty to the niceties of class distinction, and though he had cured himself of his early tendency to address the butler as 'Bill', he never failed to consult him as man to man in his moments of perplexity. Bayliss was always eager to be of assistance. He liked Mr Crocker. True, his manner might have struck a more sensitive man than his employer as a shade too closely resembling that of an indulgent father toward a son who was not quite right in the head; but it had genuine affection in it.

Mr Crocker picked up his paper and folded it back at the sporting page, pointing with a stubby forefinger.

'Well, what does all this mean? I've kept out of watching cricket since I landed in England, but yesterday they got the poison needle to work and took me off to see Surrey play Kent at that place, Lord's, where you say you go sometimes.'

'I was there yesterday, sir. A very exciting game.'

'Exciting? How do you make that out? I sat in the bleachers all afternoon waiting for something to break loose. Doesn't anything ever happen at cricket?'

The butler winced a little, but managed to smile a tolerant smile. This man, he reflected, was but an American, and as much more to be pitied than censured. He endeavoured to explain.

'It was a sticky wicket yesterday, sir, owing to the rain.'

'Eh?'

'The wicket was sticky, sir.'

'Come again.'

'I mean that the reason why the game yesterday struck you as slow was that the wicket – I should say the turf – was sticky – that is to say, wet. Sticky is the technical term, sir. When the wicket is sticky the batsmen are obliged to exercise a great deal of caution, as the stickiness of the wicket enables the bowlers to make the ball turn more sharply in either direction as it strikes the turf than when the wicket is not sticky.'

'That's it, is it?'

'Yes, sir.'

'Thanks for telling me.'

'Not at all, sir.'

Mr Crocker pointed to the paper.

'Well, now, this seems to be the boxscore of the game we saw yesterday. If you can make sense out of that, go to it.'

The passage on which his finger rested was headed Final Score, and ran as follows:

SURREY
FIRST INNINGS

Hayward, c Wooley b Carr	67
Hobbs, run out	0
Hayes, st Huish b Fielder	12
Ducat, b Fielder	33
Harrison, not out	11
Sandham, not out	6
Extras	10
Total (for four wickets)	139

Bayliss inspected the cipher gravely.

'What is it you wish me to explain, sir?'

'Why, the whole thing. What's it all about?'

'It's perfectly simple, sir. Surrey won the toss and took first knock. Hayward and Hobbs were the opening pair. Hayward called Hobbs for a short run, but the latter was unable to get across and was thrown out by mid-on. Hayes was the next man in. He went out of his ground and was stumped. Ducat and Hayward made a capital stand considering the stickiness of the wicket, until Ducat was bowled by a good length off-break and Hayward caught at second slip off a googly. Then Harrison and Sandham played out time.'

Mr Crocker breathed heavily through his nose.

'Yes!' he said. 'Yes! I had an idea that was it. But I think I'd like to have it once again slowly. Start with these figures. What does that sixty-seven mean, opposite Hayward's name?'

'He made sixty-seven runs, sir.'

'Sixty-seven! In one game?'

'Yes, sir.'

'Why, Home-Run Baker couldn't do it!'

'I am not familiar with Mr Baker, sir.'

'I suppose you've never seen a ball game?'

'Ball game, sir?'

'A baseball game?'

'Never, sir.'

'Then, Bill,' said Mr Crocker, reverting in his emotion to the bad habit of his early London days, 'you haven't lived. See here!'

Whatever vestige of respect for class distinctions Mr Crocker had managed to preserve during the opening stages of the interview now definitely disappeared. His eyes shone wildly and he snorted like a warhorse. He clutched the butler by the sleeve and drew him closer to the table, then began to move forks, spoons, cups, and even the contents of his plate, about the cloth with an energy little short of feverish.

'Bayliss?'

'Sir?'

'Watch!' said Mr Crocker, with the air of an excitable high priest about to initiate a novice into the mysteries.

He removed a roll from the basket.

'You see this roll? That's the home plate. This spoon is first base. Where I'm putting this cup is second. This piece of bacon is third. There's your diamond for you. Very well then. These lumps of sugar are the infielders and the outfielders. Now we're ready. Batter up! He stands here. Catcher behind him. Umps behind catcher.'

'Umps, I take it, sir, is what we would call the umpire?'

'Call him anything you like. It's part of the game. Now here's the box, where I've put this dab of marmalade, and here's the pitcher winding up.'

'The pitcher would be equivalent to our bowler?'

'I guess so, though why you should call him a bowler gets past me.'

'The box, then, is the bowler's wicket?'

'Have it your own way. Now pay attention. Play ball! Pitcher's winding up. Put it over, Mike, put it over! Some speed, kid! Here it comes right in the groove. Bing! Batter slams it and streaks for first. Outfielder – this lump of sugar – boots it. Bonehead! Batter touches second. Third? No! Get back! Can't be done. Play it safe. Stick round the sack, old pal. Second batter up. Pitcher getting something on the ball now besides the cover. Whiffs him. Back to the bench, Cyril! Third batter up. See him rub his hands in the dirt. Watch this kid. He's good! Lets two alone, then slams the next right on the nose. Whizzes round to second. First guy, the one we left on second, comes home for one run. That's a game! Take it from me, Bill, that's a game!'

Somewhat overcome with the energy with which he had flung himself into his lecture, Mr Crocker sat down and refreshed himself with cold coffee.

'Quite an interesting game,' said Bayliss. 'But I find, now that you have explained it, sir, that it is familiar to me, though I have always known it under another name. It is played a great deal in this country.'

Mr Crocker started to his feet.

'It is? And I've been five years here without finding it out! When's the next game scheduled?'

'It is known in England as rounders, sir. Children play it with a soft ball and a racket, and derive considerable enjoyment from it. I have never heard of it before as a pastime for adults.'

Two shocked eyes stared into the butler's face.

'Children?' The word came in a whisper. 'A racket?'

'Yes, sir.'

'You – you didn't say a soft ball?'

'Yes, sir.'

A sort of spasm seemed to convulse Mr Crocker. He had lived five years in England, but not till this moment had he realised to the full how utterly alone he was in an alien land. Fate had placed him, bound and helpless, in a country where they called baseball rounders and played it with a soft ball.

How's That, Umpire?

The story of Conky Biddle's great love begins
at about six forty-five on an evening in June in
the Marylebone district of London. He had
spent the day at Lord's cricket ground watching a cricket match, and driving away at close
of play had been held up in a traffic jam. And
held up alongside his taxi was a car with a girl
at the wheel. And he had just lit a cigarette and
was thinking of this and that, when he heard
her say:

'Cricket is not a game. It is a mere shallow
excuse for walking in your sleep.'

It was at this point that love wound its
silken fetters about Conky. He leaped like a
jumping bean and the cigarette fell from his
nerveless fingers. If a girl who talked like that
was not his dream girl, he didn't know a
dream girl when he heard one.

You couldn't exactly say that he fell in love
at first sight, for owing to the fact that in
between him and her, obscuring the visibility,
there was sitting a robust blighter in blue flannel with a pin stripe, he couldn't see her. All he
had to go on was her voice, but that was
ample. It was a charming voice with an
American intonation. She was probably, he
thought, an American angel who had stepped

down from Heaven for a short breather in London.

'If I see another cricket game five thousand years from now,' she said, 'that'll be soon enough.'

Her companion plainly disapproved of these cracks. He said in a stiff, sniffy sort of way that she had not seen cricket at its best that afternoon, play having been greatly interfered with by rain.

'A merciful dispensation,' said the girl. 'Cricket with hardly any cricket going on is a lot better than cricket where the nuisance persists uninterrupted. In my opinion the ideal contest would be one where it rained all day and the rival teams stayed home doing their crossword puzzles.'

The traffic jam then broke up and the car shot forward like a B.29, leaving the taxi nowhere.

The reason why this girl's words had made so deep an impression on the young Biddle was that of all things in existence, with the possible exception of slugs and his uncle Everard, Lord Plumpton, he disliked cricket most. As a boy he had been compelled to play it, and grown to man's estate he was compelled to watch it. And if there was one spectacle that saddened him more than another in a world where the man of sensibility is always being saddened by spectacles, it was that of human beings, the heirs of the ages, waddling about in pads and shouting 'How's that, umpire?'

He had to watch cricket because Lord Plumpton told him to, and he was dependent on the other for his three squares a day. Lord

Plumpton was a man who knew the batting averages of every first-class cricketer back to the days when they used to play in top hats and whiskers, and recited them to Conky after dinner. He liked to show Conky with the assistance of an apple (or, in winter, of an orange) how Bodger of Kent got the fingerspin which enabled him to make the ball dip and turn late on a sticky wicket. And frequently when Conky was walking along the street with him and working up to touching him for a tenner, he would break off the conversation at its most crucial point in order to demonstrate with his umbrella how Codger of Sussex made his late cut through the slips.

It was to the home of this outstanding louse, where he had a small bedroom on an upper floor, that Conky was now on his way. Arriving at journey's end, he found a good deal of stir and bustle going on, with doctors coming downstairs with black bags and parlourmaids going upstairs with basins of gruel, and learned from the butler that Lord Plumpton had sprained his ankle.

'No, really?' said Conky, well pleased, for if his uncle had possessed as many ankles as a centipede he would thoroughly have approved of him spraining them all. 'I suppose I had better go up and view the remains.'

He proceeded to the star bedroom and found his uncle propped up with pillows, throwing gruel at the parlourmaid. It was plain that he was in no elfin mood. He was looking like a mass murderer, though his face lacked the genial expression which you often see in mass murderers, and he glared at Conky with the sort of wild regret which sweeps over an irritable man when he sees a loved one approaching his sick bed and realises that he has used up all the gruel.

'What ho, Uncle Everard,' said Conky. 'The story going the round of the clubs is that you have bust a joint of sorts. What happened?'

Lord Plumpton scowled darkly. He looked now like a mass murderer whose stomach ulcers are paining him.

'I'll tell you what happened. You remember I had to leave you at Lord's to attend a committee meeting at my club. Well, as I was walking back from the club, there were some children playing cricket in the street and one of them skied the ball towards extra cover, so naturally I ran out into the road to catch it. I judged it to a nicety and had just caught it when a homicidal lunatic of a girl came blinding along at ninety miles an hour in her car and knocked me base over apex. One of these days,' said Lord Plumpton, licking his lips, 'I hope to meet that girl again, preferably down a dark alley. I shall skin her very slowly with a blunt knife, dip her in boiling oil, sever her limb from limb, assemble those limbs on the pavement and dance on them.'

'And rightly,' said Conky. 'These girls who bust your ankles and prevent you going to Lord's tomorrow need a sharp lesson.'

'What do you mean, prevent me going to Lord's tomorrow? Do you think a mere sprained ankle will stop me going to a cricket match? I shall be there, with you at my side. And now,' said Lord Plumpton, wearying of these exchanges, 'go to hell.'

Conky did not go to hell, but he went downstairs and out on to the front steps to get a breath of air. He was feeling low and depressed. He had been so certain that he would be able to get tomorrow off. He had turned to go in again when he heard a noise of brakes as a car drew up behind him.

'Excuse me,' said a voice. 'Could I see Lord Plumpton?'

Simple words, but their effect on Conky as he recognised that silvery voice was to make him quiver from stay-combed hair to shoe sole. He uttered a whinnying cry which, as he swivelled round and for the first time was privileged to see her face, became a gasp. The voice had been the voice of an angel. The face measured up to the voice.

Seeing him, she too gasped. This was apt to be the reaction of the other sex on first beholding Conky Biddle, for though his I.Q. was low his outer crust was rather sensational. He was, indeed, a dazzlingly good-looking young man, who out-Caryed Grant and began where Gregory Peck left off.

'I say,' he said, going to the car and placing a foot on the running-board. 'Don't look now, but did I by chance hear you expressing a wish to meet my uncle, Lord Plumpton?'

'That's right. I recently flattened him out with my car, and I was planning to give him some flowers.'

'I wouldn't,' said Conky. 'I really wouldn't. I say this as a friend. Time, the great healer, will have to pull up its socks and spit on its hands quite a bit before it becomes safe for you to enter the presence.'

'I see. Then I'll take the blooms around the

corner and have them delivered by a messenger boy. How's that, umpire?'

Conky winced. It was as though he had heard this divine creature sully her lips with something out of a modern historical novel.

'Good God!' he said. 'Where did you pick up that obscene expression?'

'From your uncle. He was chanting it at the top of his voice when I rammed him. A mental case, I imagine. What does it mean?'

'It's what you say at cricket.'

'Cricket!' The girl shuddered strongly. 'Shall I tell you what I think of cricket?'

'I have already heard your views. Your car got stuck abaft my taxi in a traffic block this evening. I was here, if you follow what I mean, and you were there, a few feet to the nor-nor-east, so I was able to drink in what you were saying about cricket. Would you mind if I thanked you with tears in my eyes?'

'Not at all. But don't you like cricket? I thought all Englishmen loved it.'

'Not this Englishman. It gives me the pip.'

'Me, too. I ought never to have gone near that Lord's place. But in a moment of weakness I let myself be talked into it by my *fiancé*.'

Conky reeled.

'Was he the bloke you were talking to in the car?'

'That's right. Eustace Davenport-Simms. I think he plays for Essex or Sussex or somewhere. My views were too subversive for him, so after kidding back and forth for a while we decided to cancel the order for the wedding cake.'

'I thought he seemed a bit sniffy.'

'He got sniffier.'

'Very sensible of you not to marry a crick-eter.'

'So I felt.'

'The upshot, then, when all the smoke has blown away, is that you are once more in cir-culation?'

'Yes.'

'Well, that's fine,' said Conky. A sudden thought struck him. 'I say, would you object if I pressed your little hand?'

'Some other time, I think.'

'Any time that suits you.'

'You see, I have to hie me back to my hotel and dress. I'm late already, and my father screams like a famished hyaena if he's kept waiting for his rations.'

And with a rapid thrust of her shapely foot she set the machinery in motion and vanished round the corner on two wheels, leaving Conky staring after her with a growing feeling of desolation. He had just realised that he was unaware of her name, address and telephone number and had had what was probably his last glimpse of her. If the expression 'Ships that pass in the night' had been familiar to him, he would certainly have uttered it, using clenched teeth for the purpose.

It was a Conky with heart bowed down and a general feeling of having been passed through the wringer who accompanied his uncle to Lord's next morning. The thought that a Grade A soulmate had come into his life and buzzed out again, leaving no clue to her iden-tity or whereabouts, was a singularly bitter one. Lord Plumpton on the journey to the Mecca of cricket spoke well and easily of the visit of the Australian team of 1921, but Conky proved a distrait listener, so distrait that Lord Plumpton prodded him irascibly in the ribs and called him an infernal goggle-eyed fathead, which of course he was.

He was still in a sort of trance when they took their seats in the pavilion, but here it was less noticeable, for everybody else was in a sort of trance. The somnambulists out in the field tottered to and fro, and the spectators lay back and let their eyes go glassy. For perhaps an hour nothing happened except that Hodger of Middlesex, waking like Abou ben Adhem from a deep dream of peace, flicked his bat at a rising ball and edged it into the hands of a sleeper dozing in what is technically known as the gully. Then Lord Plumpton, who had been silent except for an occasional 'Nice! Nice!' sat up with a sudden jerk and an explosive 'Well, I'm dashed!' and glared sideways at the three shilling seats which adjoined the pavilion. And Conky, following his gaze, felt his heart execute four separate buck and wing steps and come to rest quivering like a jelly in a high wind.

'Well, I'm dashed!' said Lord Plumpton, continuing to direct it at the three shilling seats the kind of look usually associated with human fiends in mystery stories. 'There's that blasted girl!'

It was not a description which Conky himself would have applied to the divinest of her sex, nor one which he enjoyed hearing applied to her, and for a moment he was in two minds as to whether to haul off and sock his relative on the beezer. Wiser counsels prevailed, and he said:

'Yes, there she spouts.'

Lord Plumpton seemed surprised.

'You know her?'

'Just slightly. She ran into me last night.'

'Into you, too? Good gad, the female's a public menace. If she's allowed to remain at large, the population of London will be decimated. I've a good mind to go over and tell her what I think of her.'

'But your uncle, ankle.'

'What the devil are you gibbering about?'

'I mean your ankle, uncle. You mustn't walk about on it. How would it be if I popped over and acquainted her with your displeasure?'

Lord Plumpton considered.

'Yes, that's not a bad idea. A surprisingly good idea, in fact, considering what a nitwit you are. But pitch it strong.'

'Oh, I will,' said Conky.

He rose and hurried off, and Lord Plumpton fell into conversation with the barely animate spectator on his left. They were soon deep in an argument as to whether it was at square leg or at extra cover that D.C.L. Wodger of Gloucestershire had fielded in 1904.

If the girl had looked like the better class of angel in the uncertain light of last night, she looked more than ever so in the reasonably bright sunshine of today. She was one of those lissom girls of medium height. Her eyes and hair were a browny hazel. The general effect was of a seraph who ate lots of yeast.

'Oh, hullo,' said Conky, lowering himself into a seat beside her. 'We meet again, what?'

She seemed surprised and startled. In her manner, as she gazed at his clean-cut face and then into his frank blue eyes, there was something that might almost be described as fluttering.

'You!' she cried. 'What are you doing here?'

'Just watching cricket.'

'But you told me last night that cricket gave you the pip, which I imagine is something roughly equivalent to the megrims or the heeby-jeebies.'

'Quite. But, you see, it's like this. My uncle is crazy about the ghastly game and I'm dependent on him, so when he says "Come along and watch cricket", I have to come along and watch it like a lynx.'

The girl frowned. It was as if she had been hurt and disappointed.

'Why are you dependent on your uncle? Why don't you get a job?'

Conky hastened to defend himself.

'I do get a job. I get dozens of jobs. But I lose them all. The trouble is, you see, that I'm not very bright.'

'No?'

'Not very. That's why they call me Conky.'

'Do they call you Conky?'

'Invariably. What started it was an observation one of the masters at school happened to drop one day. He said, addressing me – "To attempt to drive information into your head, Biddle, is no easy task, for Providence, mysterious in its workings, has given you instead of the more customary human brain a skull full of concrete." So after that everyone called me Conky.'

'I see. What sort of jobs have you tried?'

'Practically everything except Chancellor of the Duchy of Lancaster.'

'And you get fired every time?'

'Every time.'

'I'm sorry.'

'It's dashed white of you to be sorry, but as a matter of fact it's all right.'

'How do you mean it's all right?'

Conky hesitated. Then he reflected that if you couldn't confide in an angel in human shape, who could you confide in? He glanced about him. Except for themselves, the three shilling tier of seats was almost empty.

'Well, you'll keep it under your hat, won't you, because it's supposed to be very hush-hush at the moment. I am on the eve of making a stupendous fortune. You know sea water?'

'The stuff that props the ship up when you come over from New York?'

'That's right. Well, you probably aren't aware of it, but it's full of gold, and I'm in with a fellow who's got a secret process for scooping it out. I saw his advertisement in the paper saying that if you dashed along and brassed up quick you could get in on an invention of vast possibilities, so I dashed along and brassed up. He was a nice chap and let me into the thing without a murmur. Bloke of the name of MacSporran. I happened to have scraped up ten quid, so I put that in and he tells me that at a conservative estimate I shall get back about two hundred and fifty thousand. I call that a nice profit.'

'Very nice.'

'Yes, it's all very convenient. And when I

say that, I'm not thinking so much of the jolliness of having all that splosh in the old sock, I am alluding more to the difference this has made in what you might call my matrimonial plans. If I want to get married, I mean. What I'm driving at,' said Conky, giving her a melting look, 'is that I am now in a position, when I meet the girl I love, to put the binge on a practical basis.'

'I see.'

'In fact,' said Conky, edging a little closer. 'I might almost start making my plans at once.'

'That's the spirit. Father's slogan is "Do it now", and he's a tycoon.'

'I thought a tycoon was a sort of storm.'

'No, a millionaire.'

'Is your father a millionaire?'

'Yes, and more pouring in all the time.'

'Oh?'

A sudden chill had come over Conky's dashing mood. The one thing he had always vowed he would never do was marry for money. For years his six uncles and seven aunts has been urging him to cash in on his looks and grab something opulent. They had paraded heiresses before him in droves, but he had been firm. He had his principles.

Of course, in the present case it was different. He loved this girl with every fibre of his being. But all the same . . . No, he told himself, better wait till his bank balance was actually bulging.

With a strong effort he changed the conversation.

'Well, as I was saying,' he said, 'I hope to clean up shortly on an impressive scale, and when I do I'll never watch another cricket match as long as I live. Arising from which, what on earth are you doing here, holding the views on cricket which you do?'

A slight shadow of disappointment seemed to pass over the girl's face. It was as if she had been expecting the talk to develop along different lines.

'Oh, I came for a purpose.'

'Eh? What purpose?'

She directed his attention to the rows of living corpses in the pavilion. Lord Plumpton and his friend, having settled the Wodger question, were leaning back with their hats over their eyes. It was difficult to realise that life still animated those rigid limbs.

'When I was here yesterday, I was greatly struck by the spectacle of those stiffs over there. I wondered if it was possible to stir them up into some sort of activity.'

'I doubt it.'

'I'm a little dubious myself. They're like fish on a slab or a Westminster matinee audience. Still, I thought I would try. Yesterday, of course I hadn't elastic and ammo with me.'

'Elastic? Ammo?'

Conky stared. From the recesses of her costume she had produced a piece of stout elastic and a wad of tin foil. She placed the tin foil on the elastic and then between her teeth. Then, turning, she took careful aim at Lord Plumpton.

For a sighting shot it was an admirable effort. Conky, following the projectile with a rapt gaze, saw his uncle start and put a hand to his ear. There seemed little reason to doubt that he had caught it amidships.

'Good Lord!' he cried. 'Here, after you with that elastic. I used to do that at school, and many was the fine head I secured. I wonder if the old skill still lingers.'

It was some minutes later that Lord Plumpton turned to the friend beside him.

'Wasps very plentiful this year,' he said.

The friend blinked drowsily.

'Watts?'

'Wasps.'

'There was A.R.K. Watts who used to play for Sussex. Ark we used to call him.'

'Not Watts. Wasps.'

'Wasps?'

'Wasps.'

'What about them?'

'They seem very plentiful. One stung me in the ear just now. And now one of them has knocked off my hat. Most extraordinary.'

A man in a walrus moustache who had played for Surrey in 1911 came along, and Lord Plumpton greeted him cordially.

'Hullo, Freddie.'

'Hullo.'

'Good game.'

'Very. Exciting.'

'Wasps are a nuisance, though.'

'Wasps?'

'Wasps.'

'What wasps?'

'I don't know their names. The wasps around here.'

'No wasps around here.'

'Yes.'

'Not in the pavilion at Lord's. You can't get in unless you're a member.'

'Well, one has just knocked off my hat. And look, there goes Jimmy's hat.'

The walrus shook his head. He stooped and picked up a piece of tin toil.

'Someone's shooting this stuff at you. Used to do it myself a long time ago. Ah yes,' he said, peering about him, 'I see where the stuff's coming from. That girl over there in the three shilling seats with your nephew. If you look closely, you'll see she's drawing a bead on you now.

Lord Plumpton looked, startled and stiffened.

'That girl again! Is one to be beset by her through all eternity? Send for the attendants! Rouse the attendants and give them their divisional orders. Instruct the attendants to arrest her immediately and bring her to the committee room.'

And so it came about that just as Conky was adjusting the elastic to his lips a short while later and preparing to loose off, a heavy hand fell on his shoulder, and there was a stern-faced man in the uniform of a Marylebone Cricket Club attendant. And simultaneously another heavy hand fell on the girl's shoulder, and there was another stern-faced man in the uniform of another Marylebone Cricket Club attendant.

It was a fair cop.

The committee room of the Marylebone Cricket Club is a sombre and impressive apartment. Photographs of bygone cricketers, many of them with long beards, gaze down from the walls – accusingly, or so it seems to the man whose conscience is not as clear as it might be. Only a man with an exceptionally clear conscience can enter this holy of holies without feeling that he is about to be stripped of his MCC tie and formally ticketed as a social leper.

This is particularly so when, as in the present instance the President himself is seated at his desk. It was at Lord Plumpton's request that he was there now. It had seemed to Lord Plumpton that a case of this magnitude could be dealt with adequately only at the very highest levels.

He mentioned this in his opening speech for the prosecution.

'I demand,' said Lord Plumpton, 'the most exemplary punishment for an outrage unparalleled in the annals of the Marylebone Cricket Club, the dear old club we all love so well, if you know what I mean.' Here he paused as if intending to bare his head, but realising that he had not got his hat on, continued, 'I mean to say, taking pot-shots at members with a series of slabs of tin foil, dash it! If that isn't a nice bit of box fruit, what is? Bad enough, if you see what I'm driving at, to take pot-shots at even the *cannaille*, as they call them in France, who squash in in the free seats, but when it comes to pot-shotting members in the pavilion, I mean where are we? Personally I would advocate skinning the girl, but if you consider that too extreme I am prepared to settle for twenty years in solitary confinement. A menace to the community, that's what this girl is. Busting about in her car and knocking people endways with one hand and flicking their hats off with the other, if you follow my drift. She reminds me of . . . who was that woman in the Bible whose work was always so raw? . . . Delilah? . . . No . . . It's on the tip of my tongue . . . Ah yes, Jezebel. She's a modern streamlined Jezebel, dash her insides.'

'Uncle Everard,' said Conky, 'you are speaking of the woman I love.'

The girl gave a little gasp.

'No, really?' she said.

'Absolutely,' said Conky. 'I had intended to mention it earlier. I don't know your name . . .'

'Clarissa. Clarissa Binstead.'

'How many s's?'

'Three, if you count the Binstead.'

'Clarissa, I love you. Will you be my wife?'

'Sure,' said the girl. 'I was hoping you'd suggest it. And what all the fuss is about is more than I can understand. Why when we go to a ball game in America, we throw pop bottles.'

There was a silence.

'Are you an American, madam?' said the President.

'One hundred per cent. Oh, say, can you see . . . No, I never can remember how it goes after that. I could whistle it for you.'

The President had drawn Lord Plumpton aside. His face was grave and anxious.

'My dear Everard,' he said in an urgent undertone, 'we must proceed carefully here, very carefully. I had no notion this girl was American. Somebody should have informed me. The last thing we want is an international incident, particularly at a moment when we are hoping, if all goes well, to get into America's ribs for a bit of the stuff. I can fully appreciate your wounded feelings . . .'

'And how about my wounded topper?'

'The club will buy you a new hat, and then, my dear fellow, I would strongly urge that we consider the matter closed.'

'You mean not skin her?'

'No.'

'Not slap her into the cooler for twenty years?'

'No. There might be very unfortunate repercussions.'

'Oh, all right,' said Lord Plumpton sullenly. 'Oh, very well. But,' he proceeded on a brighter note, 'there is one thing I can do, and that is disinherit this frightful object here. Hoy!' he said to Conky.

'Hullo?' said Conky.

'You are no longer a nephew of mine.'

'Well, that's a bit of goose,' said Conky.

As he came out of the committee room, he was informed by an attendant that a gentleman wished to speak to him on the telephone. Excusing himself to Clarissa and bidding her wait for him downstairs Conky went to the instrument, listened for a few moments, then reeled away, his eyes bulging and his jaw a-droop. He found Clarissa at the spot agreed upon.

'Hullo, there,' said Conky. 'I say, you remember me asking you to be my wife?'

'Yes.'

'You said you would.'

'Yes.'

'Well, the words that spring to the lips are "*Will* you?" Because I'm afraid the whole thing's off. That was MacSporran on the 'phone. He said he'd made a miscalculation, and my tenner won't be enough to start that sea water scheme going. He said he would need another thirty thousand pounds and could I raise it? I said No, and he said "Too bad, too bad." And I said: "Do I get my tenner back?", and he said "No, you don't get your tenner back." So there you are. I can't marry you.'

Clarissa wrinkled her forehead.

'I don't see it. Father's got it in gobs. He will provide.'

'Not for me, he won't. I always swore I'd never marry a girl for her money.'

'You aren't marrying me for my money. You're marrying me because we're soul-mates.'

'That's true. Still, you appear to have a most ghastly lot of the stuff, and I haven't a bean.'

'Suppose you had a job?'

'Oh, if I had a job.'

'That's all right, then. Father runs a gigantic business and he can always find room for another Vice-President.'

'Vice-President?'

'Yes.'

'But I don't know enough to be a Vice-President.'

'It's practically impossible not to know enough to be a Vice-President. All you would have to do would be to attend conferences and say "Yes" when Father made a suggestion.'

'What in front of a whole lot of people?'

'Well, at least you could nod.'

'Oh yes, I could nod.'

'Then that's settled. Kiss me.'

Their lips met long and lingeringly. Conky

came out of the clinch with sparkling eyes and a heightened colour. He raised a hand to heaven.

'How's that, umpire?' he cried.

'Jolly good show, sir,' said Clarissa.

Reginald's
Record Knock

Reginald Humby was one of those men who go in just above the byes, and are to tired bowlers what the dew is to parched earth at the close of an August afternoon. When a boy at school he once made nine not out in a house match, but after that he went all to pieces. His adult cricket career was on the one-match one-ball principle. Whether it was that Reginald hit too soon at them or did not hit soon enough, whether it was that his bat deviated from the dotted line which joined the two points A and B in the illustrated plate of the man making the forward stroke in the *Hints on Cricket* book, or whether it was that each ball swerved both ways at once and broke a yard and a quarter, I do not know. Reginald rather favoured the last theory.

The important point is that Reginald, after an almost unbroken series of eggs in the first two months of the season, turned out for Chigley Heath versus The Hearty Lunchers in the early part of July, went in first, and knocked up a hundred and thirteen.

Reginald, mark you, whose normal batting style was a sort of cross between hop-scotch, diabolo, and a man with gout in one leg trying to dance the Salomé Dance.

When great events happen the public generally shows an anxiety to discover their cause. In the case of Reginald's century, on the face of it the most remarkable event since the Flood, the miracle may be attributed directly to his personal popularity.

Carpers may cavil at this statement. It is possible, too, that cavillers may carp. I seem to see them at it. All around me, I repeat, I seem to hear the angry murmur of carpers cavilling and cavillers carping. I seem to hear them asking how it is possible for a man to make a century by being popular.

'Can a batsman,' they ask, 'by sheer amiability stop a yorker on the leg stump?'

Nevertheless it is true. The facts are these:

Everybody who plays club cricket knows the Hearty Lunchers. Inveterate free-drinkers to a man, they wander about the country playing villages. They belong to the school of thought which holds that the beauty of cricket is that, above all other games, it offers such magnificent opportunities for a long drink and a smoke in the shade. The Hearty Lunchers do not take their cricket in that spirit of deadly and business-like earnest which so many people consider is spoiling the game. A Hearty Luncher who has been given out caught at the wicket does not explain on arriving at the pavilion that he was nowhere near the ball, and that the umpire has had a personal grudge against him since boyhood. No, he sinks into a deck chair, removes his pads, and remarks that if anyone was thinking of buying him a stone ginger with the merest dash of gin in it, now is his time.

It will therefore readily be understood that

Reginald's inability to lift his average out of the minuses did not handicap him with the Hearty Lunchers, as it might have handicapped him with some clubs. The genial sportsmen took him to their bosoms to a man and looked on him as a brother. Reginald's was one of those noble natures which are always good for five shillings at any hour of the day, and the Hearty Lunchers were not slow to appreciate it. They all loved Reginald.

Reginald was seated in his room one lovely evening at the beginning of July oiling a bat – he was a confirmed bat-oiler – when the telephone bell rang. He went to the instrument and was hailed by the comfortable voice of Westaway, the Hearty Lunchers' secretary.

'Is that Humby?' asked Westaway. 'I say, Reggie, I'm booking you for the Chigley Heath match next Saturday. Train, Waterloo, ten fifteen.'

'Oh, I say,' replied Reginald, a note of penitence in his voice, 'I'm afraid I can't – fact is, I'm playing for Chigley.'

'You're what?'

'They asked me last week – they seemed very keen that I should play.'

'Why, haven't they seen you play?'

'I'm awfully sorry.'

'Oh, all right. How do you come to be mixed up with Chigley Heath?'

'My *fiancée* lives down there.'

'I see. Well, so long.'

'So long.'

'You're all right for the Saturday after against Porkley-in-the-Wold, I suppose?'

'Yes, rather!'

'Good! So long.'

'So long.'

And Reginald, replacing the instrument, resumed the oiling of the bat.

Now Westaway happened to be of a romantic and sentimental nature. He was inclined to be stout, and all rather stout men are sentimental. Westaway was the sort of man who keeps old ball-programmes and bundles of letters tied round with lilac ribbon. At country houses, when they lingered on the terrace after dinner to watch the moonlight flooding the quiet garden, it was Westaway and his colleagues who lingered longest. Westaway knew Tennyson's 'Maud' by heart, and could take Browning without gas.

It is not to be wondered at, therefore, that Reginald's remark about his *fiancée* living at Chigley Heath should give him food for thought. It appealed to him.

He reflected on it a good deal during the evening, and running across Blagdon, the Hearty Lunchers' captain, after dinner that night at the Club, he spoke of the matter to him. It so happened that both had dined excellently and were looking on the world with a sort of cosy benevolence. They were in the mood when men give small boys sixpences.

'I rang up Reggie Humby today,' said Westaway.

'One of the best, Reggie,' said Blagdon. 'Waiter, coffee and – what's yours? Coffee for two, a Maraschino, a liqueur brandy, and two of those old-shape Larranagas. Yes, dear old chap, Reggie.'

'Did you know he was engaged?'

'I did hear something about it – girl of the name of Belleville or something like that –

Melville, that's it! Charming girl. Fond of poetry and all that, I believe.'

'She lives at Chigley Heath.'

'Then Reggie'll get a chance of seeing her next Saturday.'

'He tells me he's promised to play for Chigley Heath against us.'

'Confound him, the renegade! Still, we needn't scratch because of that, need we?'

Westaway sucked at his cigar in silence for a while, watching with dreamy eyes the blue smoke as it curled ceilingwards. When he spoke his voice was singularly soft.

'Do you know, Blagdon,' he said, sipping his Maraschino with a sort of gentle melancholy, 'do you know, there is something wonderfully pathetic to me in this business, I see the whole thing so clearly. There was a kind of quiver in poor Reggie's voice when he said: "I am playing for Chigley Heath, my *fiancée* lives down there," which told me more than any words could have done. It is a tragedy in its way, Blagdon. We may smile at it, think it trivial; but it is none the less a tragedy. That warm-hearted, enthusiastic girl, all eagerness to see the man she loves do well. Reggie, poor old Reggie, all on fire to prove to her that her trust in him is not misplaced, and the end – Disillusionment – Disappointment – Unhappiness.'

'He might be duck not out,' said the more practical Blagdon.

'He won't go in last for Chigley Heath; probably they think a lot of him. He may be their hope. Quite possibly he may go in first.'

'If Reggie's mug enough to let himself be shoved in first,' said Blagdon decidedly, 'he deserves all he gets. Waiter, two whiskies and soda, large.'

Westaway was in no mood to subscribe to this stony-hearted view.

'I tell you,' he said, 'I'm *sorry* for Reggie! I'm *sorry* for the poor old chap, and I'm more than sorry for the girl.'

'Well, I don't see what we can do,' said Blagdon. 'Not all the soda, thanks. We can hardly be expected to bowl badly just to let Reggie show off before his girl.'

Westaway paused in the act of lighting his cigar, as one smitten with a great thought.

'Why not?' he said. 'Why not, Blagdon? Blagdon, you've hit it!'

'My dear chap!'

'You have! I tell you, Blagdon, you've solved the whole thing. Reggie's a dashed good sort, one of the very absolute! Why not give him a benefit? Why not let him knock up a few for a change? It'll be the only chance he'll ever get of making a decent score. You aren't going to tell me at your time of life that you care whether we beat Chigley Heath or not!'

'I was thinking more of the dashing about in a hot sun while Reggie made his runs – I'm all against too much exercise.'

Blagdon was one of the non-stooping brigade. He liked best to field point with a good cover behind him.

'Oh, nonsense!' said Westaway; 'there won't be too much of that, we can be getting the rest of them out all the while; and, besides, fifty will satisfy poor old Reggie. We needn't let him make a hundred.'

Blagdon's benevolence was expanding

under the influence of the whisky and soda (large) and the old-shaped Larranaga. Little acts of kindness on Reggie's part, here a cigar, there a lunch, at another time a box at a theatre, began to rise to the surface of his memory like rainbow-coloured bubbles. Having grown accustomed to the basic bizarreness of the hon. secretary's idea, he began now, as it were, to out-Westaway Westaway.

'No!' he said, 'let us do the thing in style. Reggie shall have his knock and he shall make a century, unless, of course, they put him in last. If they do that he will have to be satisfied with twenty or so.'

'As to squaring the bowlers,' said Westaway, 'can that be managed?'

'You and I will go on first, with Blake and Harris as first change. After Blake and Harris, Grigson can have an over, too. We will broach the matter to them at a dinner at which we will be joint hosts. They are all stout fellows who will be charmed to do a little thing like this for a sportsman like Reggie.'

'Yours is a noble nature, Blagdon,' said Westaway, reaching out for his glass.

'Oh, no,' said the paragon modestly. 'Have another cigar?'

In order that the reader may get the mental strangle-hold on the plot of this narrative which is so essential if a short story is to charm, elevate, and instruct, it is necessary now for the nonce (but only for the nonce) to inspect Reginald's past life.

Reginald, as stated by Blagdon, was engaged to a Miss Melville – Miss Margaret

Melville. How few men, dear reader, are engaged to girls with svelte figures, brown hair, and large blue eyes, now sparkling and vivacious, now dreamy and soulful, but always large and blue! How few, I say. You are, dear reader, and so am I, but who else? Reginald, however, happened to be, and he considered himself uncommonly fortunate.

He was happy. It is true that Margaret's mother was not, as it were, wrapped up in him. She exhibited none of that effervescent joy at his appearance which we like to see in our mothers-in-law elect. On the contrary, she generally cried bitterly whenever she saw him, and at the end of ten minutes was apt to retire sobbing to her room, where she remained in a state of semi-coma till an advanced hour. She was by way of being a confirmed invalid, and something about Reginald seemed to get right in amongst her nerve centres, reducing them for the time being to a complicated hash. She did not like Reginald; she said she liked big, manly men. Behind his back she not infrequently referred to him as a 'poop'; sometimes even as 'that guffin.'

She did not do this to Margaret, for Margaret, besides being blue-eyed, was also a shade quick-tempered. Whenever she discussed Reginald, it was with her son Brewster. Brewster Melville, who thought Reginald a bit of an ass, was always ready to sit and listen to his mother on the subject, it being, however, an understood thing that at the conclusion of the séance she yielded one or two minted sovereigns towards his racing debts. For Brewster, having developed a habit of backing horses which either did not start at all or else sat down and thought in the middle of a race, could always do with a pound or two. His prices for these interviews worked out, as a rule, at about two and a half guineas a thousand words.

In these circumstances it is not to be wondered at that Reginald and Margaret should prefer to meet, when they did meet, at some other spot than the latter's ancestral home. It suited both of them better that they should arrange a secret tryst each week. Reginald preferred it because being in the same room as Mrs Melville always made him feel like a murderer with particularly large feet; and Margaret preferred it because, as she told Reginald, these secret meetings lent a touch of poetry, a sort of atmosphere of Marcus Stone's pictures, to what might otherwise have been a commonplace engagement.

Reginald thought this charming; but at the same time he could not conceal from himself the fact that Margaret's passion for the poetic cut, as it were, both ways. He admired and loved the loftiness of her soul, but, on the other hand, it was the deuce of a business having to live up to it. For Reginald was a very ordinary young man. They had tried to inoculate him with a love of Poetry at school, but it had never 'taken'. Until he was twenty-six he had been satisfied to class all poetry (except that of Mr Doss Chiderdoss) under the heading of Rot. Then he met Margaret, and the trouble began. On the day he first met her, at a picnic, she had looked so soulful, so aloof from this world, that he had felt instinctively that here was a girl who expected more from a man than a mere statement that the weather was rippin'. It so chanced that he knew just one quotation from the Classics, to wit, Tennyson's critique of the Island Valley of Avilion. He knew this because he had had the passage to write out one hundred and fifty times at school, on the occasion of his being caught smoking by a master who happened to be a passionate admirer of *The Idylls of the King.*

A remark of Margaret's that it was a splendid day for a picnic and that the country looked nice gave him his opportunity.

'It reminds me,' he said, 'of the Island Valley of Avilion, where falls not hail or rain or any snow, nor ever wind blows loudly; but it lies Deep-meadow'd, happy, fair, with orchard lawns. . . .'

He broke off here to squash a wasp; but Margaret had heard enough.

'Are you fond of poetry, Mr Humby?' she said, with a sort of far-off look.

'Er – oh, *rather!* I should think so!' said Reginald.

And that was how all the trouble had started. It had meant unremitting toil for Reginald. He felt that he had set himself a standard from which he must not fall. He bought every new volume of poetry which was praised in the Press, and learned the reviews of it by heart. Every evening he read painfully a portion of the Classics. He plodded through the poetry sections of *Bartlett's Book of Quotations*. Margaret's devotion to the various bards was so enthusiastic, and her reading so wide, that there were times when Reginald wondered if he could stand the strain. But he pegged away manfully.

He was helped by the fact that he actually

saw Margaret but rarely. Being in a government office he found it impossible to get away during the week, Chigley Heath being a matter of thirty miles or so from London. Sunday was, as a rule, the only day on which they met; and studious application to the poets during the week always enabled him to acquit himself with credit.

But the strain was fearful.

It occurred to Reginald on this particular Saturday that he was in a position to bring off a double event. The Hearty Lunchers' match was to begin at eleven-thirty. Consequently, if he arranged to meet Margaret at their usual Sunday meeting-place – Brown's boathouse, which was about a mile from the cricket-field – at four-thirty, he could have his game and still have plenty of time to pull her up the river to their favourite honeysuckled cottage for tea. If his side happened to be fielding at four o'clock he could get a substitute to act for him; and if Chigley Heath batted last he would get his captain to put him in early, so that he could get his innings over in good time.

Having laid these plans he caught his train on the Saturday morning with a light heart.

All went well from the start. The day was fine, the sun warm but tempered with a light breeze. The Hearty Lunchers batted first and lost six wickets before the interval for a hundred and twenty. The Chigley Heath crowd, mainly composed of small boys and octogenarians, who looked on the Hearty Lunchers as a first-class team because they wore bright blazers, were loud in their approval of their bowlers' performance in dismissing more than half the side for so few runs.

Reginald, who quite inadvertently had caught a hot catch at mid-on, went into the pavilion thoroughly pleased with himself. It was a red-letter day for him when he caught a catch, and this had been a particularly smart one. Indeed, he had not realised that the ball was coming in his direction at all till it hit him in the stomach.

At the festive board the Hearty Lunchers, as usual, justified their name, and it was not until a quarter to three that the match was resumed. The Hearty Lunchers believed in scientific stoking preparatory to the strenuous toil of the afternoon. The bill of fare was good and varied, and the only bitter drop in Reginald's cup was that he could not find his tobacco pouch. He had had it with him in the train, but now it had vanished. This rather saddened Reginald, for the pouch had been given to him by Margaret, and he had always thought it one more proof of the way her nature towered over the natures of other girls, that she had not woven a monogram on it in forget-me-nots. This record pouch, I say, was missing, and Reginald mourned for the loss.

He was still moody when the team went out to the field.

The remaining Hearty Lunchers did not offer very much resistance to the Chigley Heath fast bowler, and the whole side was out with the addition of forty runs.

It was now half-past three, and Reginald saw that if he was to do himself justice with the bat he must be put in early. Buttonholing the Chigley Heath captain he explained this to him, and the captain, a sympathetic soul, requested Reginald to get his pads on and come in first with him.

Having received one favour Reginald did not like to ask another, so greatly against his will he prepared himself to take first ball. He did this with grave care. Everyone who has seen Reginald Humby bat knows that his taking of guard is one of the most impressive sights ever witnessed on the cricket field. He tilted his cap over his eyes, waggled his bat about till the umpire was satisfied that he had got two-leg, scratched the crease with a bail, looked round at the field, walked out of his ground to pat down a blade of grass, picked up a fragment of mud, waved imperatively to two small boys who looked as if they might get behind the bowler's arm, and finally settled himself, left toe well in the air, to receive the first ball.

It was then that he noted for the first time that the bowler was Blagdon.

The sight sent a thrill through Reginald. He had seen Blagdon bowl at the nets, but he had never dared to hope that he might bat against him in a match. Exigencies of space forbid a detailed description of Blagdon's bowling. Suffice it to say that it was a shade inferior as bowling to Reginald's batting as batting.

It was Reginald's invariable custom to play forward, on principle, to each ball of his first over wherever it pitched. He called this playing himself in. In accordance with this rule he lunged grandly for six balls (three of which were long-hops to leg), and Blagdon registered a maiden. Four small boys near the pavilion clapped tentatively, but an octogenarian scowled, and, having said that cricket was a brighter game in his young days, went on to compare Reginald unfavourably with Alfred Mynn.

Scarcely had Reginald recovered from the pleasurable shock of finding Blagdon bowling at one end when he was amazed to find that Westaway was bowling at the other. Critics had often wrangled warmly as to the comparative merits of Blagdon and Westaway as bowlers; some thought that Blagdon had it, others that Westaway was the more putrid of the two; a third party called it a dead heat.

The Chigley Heath captain hit Westaway's first ball for three, and Reginald, coming to the batting end, suddenly resolved that this was an occasion on which conventional rules might be flung to the winds; instead, therefore, of playing forward at a full-pitch to leg, he waited for it, and lashing out sent it flying over short slip's head for a single.

That stroke marked an epoch. Reginald was now set.

The ordinary batsman, whose average always pans out at the end of the season between the twenties and the thirties, does not understand the whirl of mixed sensations which the really incompetent cricketer experiences on the rare occasions when he does notch a few. As ball follows ball, and he does not get out, a wild exhilaration surges through him, followed by a sort of awe as if he were doing something wrong, even irreligious. Then all these yeasty emotions subside, and are blended into one glorious sensation of grandeur and majesty, as of a giant among pygmies. This last state of mind does not come till the batsman's score has passed thirty.

By the time that Reginald, ballooning one of Blagdon's half-volleys over cover-point's head, had made his score thirty-two, he was in the full grip of this feeling. As he stood patting the pitch and waiting for the ball to be returned from the boundary, he felt that this was Life, that till now he had been a mere mollusc. His eye rolled proudly round the field.

As it did so it was caught by the clock of the adjacent church, and the sight of that clock was like a douche of cold water. The hands stood at a quarter past four.

Let us pause and ponder on this point for a while. Do not let us dismiss it as if it were some mere trivial everyday difficulty, because it is not. It is about the heftiest soul problem ever handed out to suffering man. You, dear reader, play a long and stylish innings every time you go to the wickets, and so do I; but Reginald was not like us. This was the first occasion on which the ball had seemed larger to him than a rather under-sized marble. It was the first occasion on which he had ever hit at a ball with the chances in his favour of getting it anywhere near the centre of the bat.

On the other hand, he was passionately devoted to Margaret Melville, whom he was due to meet at Brown's boathouse at four-thirty sharp. It was now four-fifteen, and Brown's boathouse was still a mile away.

Reginald Humby was at the cross-roads.

The mental struggle was brief but keen. A sharp pang, and his mind was made up. Cost what it might he must stay at the wickets. Not even for Margaret could he wilfully put an end to an innings like this. If she broke off the engagement – well, it might be that Time would heal the wound, and that after many years he would find some other girl for whom he might come to care in a wrecked, broken sort of way. But a chance like this, a chance of batting, thoroughly set, against the bowling of Blagdon, Westaway, Blake, and Harris, could never come again. Such things did not happen twice in a lifetime. Only to the very favoured did they happen once. What is Love compared to a chance of knocking up a really big score? . . . Reginald prepared to face the bowling again.

Soon a burst of applause from the pavilion signalled the fact that Reginald had made the first fifty of his life.

The time was now twenty-five to five, and Brown's boathouse was exactly where it had been at a quarter past four, a mile away.

But there was no room now in Reginald's mind for even a passing thought about Brown's boathouse, for his gleaming eyes had seen that Grigson was being put on to bowl. Antony would have forgotten Cleopatra if he had had the chance of batting against Grigson.

If Grigson, as a bowler, had one fault more than another (which his friends denied), it was that he was too tantalising. In pace his deliveries were – from a batsman's point of view – ideal. It was in direction that they erred. His first ball soared languidly into the hands of second slip, without touching terra firma. His second was fielded and returned by point. Reginald watched these truants with growing impatience.

At the third ball he could restrain himself

no longer. The sight of the square-leg umpire shaping for a catch maddened him. He bounded from his crease, pushed the official to one side, and was just in time at the end of this manoevre to smite the ball as it bounced and send it hurtling to the pavilion. There were cheers; the octogenarian who had compared him to his disadvantage with Alfred Mynn handsomely retracted his words; and two small boys in their enthusiasm fell out of a tree.

Of the remaining hour and ten minutes of his innings Reginald's recollections are like some blurred but beautiful dream. He remembers occasional outstanding hits – as when he scored a boundary off a ball of Grigson's which stopped dead two-thirds of the way down the pitch, and when he beat short-slip in a race for a delivery of Harris's. But the greater part of the innings has fled from him.

One moment, however, still stands out sharp and clear in his memory – the moment when a second burst of cheering, beside which the first was as nothing, informed him that his score had reached three figures. After that one or two more lofty hits, and finally the crash of the stumps and the triumphant return to the pavilion on the shoulders of a mixed bevy of Chigley Heathens and Hearty Lunchers.

For some fifteen minutes he sat on a bench in a moist, happy trance.

And then, suddenly, like a cold douche, came the thought of Margaret.

Reginald sprang for the dressing-room and changed his clothes, his brain working feverishly.

And as he laced his boots there came, like

some knell, the sound of the clock outside striking six.

Margaret and her mother were seated in the drawing-room when Reginald arrived. Mrs Melville, who had elicited the information that Reginald had not kept his appointment, had been saying 'I told you so' for some time, and this had not improved Margaret's temper. When, therefore, Reginald, damp and dishevelled, was shown in, he felt like a man who has suddenly discovered the North Pole. Mrs Melville did her celebrated imitation of the Gorgon, while Margaret, lightly humming an air, picked up a weekly paper and became absorbed in it.

'Margaret, let me explain,' panted Reginald.

Mrs Melville was understood to remark that she dared say.

Margaret's attention was riveted by a fashion plate.

'Driving in a taximeter to Charing Cross this afternoon,' resumed Reginald, 'I had an accident.'

(Which was the net result of his feverish brain-work in the pavilion dressing-room.)

The weekly periodical flapped to the floor.

'Oh, Reggie, are you hurt?'

'A few scratches, nothing more; but it made me miss my train.'

'Oh, Reggie! but why didn't you wire? I have been worrying so.'

'I was too agitated, dearest.'

'What train did you catch?'

'The five-one.'

'Why, Brewster was coming home by the

five-one. Did you see him?'

Reginald's jaw dropped slightly.

'Er – no,' he said.

'How curious,' said Margaret.

'Very curious,' said Reginald.

'Most curious,' said Mrs Melville.

They were still reflecting on the singularity of this fact when the door opened again, and the son of the house entered in person.

'Thought I should find you here, Humby,' he said. 'They gave me this at the station to give to you; you dropped it this morning when you got out of the train.'

He handed Reginald the missing pouch.

'Thanks,' said the latter, huskily. 'When you say this morning, of course you mean this evening but thanks, all the same – thanks – thanks.'

'No, Reginald Humby, he does *not* mean this evening,' said Mrs Melville. 'Brewster, speak! From what train did that guf– did Mr Humby alight when he dropped the tobacco pouch?'

'The ten-fifteen, the porter chap told me – said he would have given it back to him then only he nipped off in the deuce of a hurry in a cab.'

Six eyes focused themselves upon Reginald.

'Margaret,' he said, 'I will not try to deceive you –'

'You may try,' observed Mrs Melville, 'but you will not succeed.'

'Well, Reginald?'

Reginald fingered his collar.

'There was no taximeter accident.'

'Ah!' said Mrs Melville.

'The fact is, I've been playing cricket for Chigley Heath against the Hearty Lunchers.'

Margaret uttered an exclamation of surprise.

'Playing cricket!'

Reginald bowed his head with manly resignation.

'Why didn't you tell me? Why didn't you arrange for us to meet on the ground? I wanted to watch the match, only I couldn't get there in the morning, and it didn't seem worth it for such a little while in the afternoon.'

Reginald was amazed.

'You take an interest in cricket, Margaret? You! I thought you scorned it, considered it an unintellectual game.'

'Why, I play regularly in the ladies' match.'

'Margaret! Why didn't you tell me?'

'I thought you might not like it. You were so spiritual, so poetic. I feared you would despise me.'

Reginald took a step forward. His voice was tense and trembling.

'Margaret,' he said, and his accents thrilled with a dawning hope, 'this is no time for misunderstandings. We must be open with one another. Our happiness is at stake. Tell me honestly, *do* you like poetry really?'

Margaret hesitated, then answered bravely:

'No, Reginald,' she said. 'It is as you suspect. I am not worthy of you. I do *not* like poetry. Ah, you shudder! You turn away!'

'I don't,' yelled Reginald. 'I *don't*. You've made me another man, Margaret!'

She stared, wild-eyed, astonished.

'What! Do you mean that you, too –'

'I should jolly well think I do. I tell you I hate the beastly stuff. I only pretended to like it because I thought you did. The hours I've spent mugging it up! I wonder I've not got brain fever.'

'Reggie! Used you to read it up too? Oh, if I'd only known!'

'And you forgive me – this afternoon, I mean?'

'Of course. You couldn't leave a cricket match. By the way, did you make any runs?'

Reginald coughed.

'A few,' he said, modestly. 'One or two. In fact, rather a lot. As a matter of fact, I made a hundred and thirteen.'

'A hundred and thirteen!' whispered Margaret. 'My hero!'

'You won't be wanting me for a bit, will you?' asked Brewster, nonchalantly. 'Think I'll smoke a cigarette in the garden.'

And sobs from the staircase told that Mrs Melville was already on her way to her room.

Ladies and Gentlemen
v. Players

Quite without meaning it, I really won the Gentlemen *v.* Players match the summer I was eighteen. They don't say anything about me in the reports, but all the time I was really the thingummy – the iron hand behind the velvet glove, or something. That's not it, but it's something of that sort. What I mean is, if it hadn't been for me, the Gentlemen would never have won. My cousin Bill admits this, and he made a century, so he ought to know.

I cut the report of the match out of the *Telegraph*. The part where I come into it begins like this: '. . . After lunch, however, a complete change came over the game. A change frequently comes over a game of cricket after lunch; but it is usually to the disadvantage of the batting side. In this case, however, the reverse happened. Up to the interval the Gentlemen, who had gone in to make three hundred and fourteen in the fourth innings of the match, had succeeded in compiling one hundred and ten, losing in the process the valuable wickets of Fry, Jackson, Spooner, and MacLaren. As N.A. Knox, who had been sent in first on the previous evening to play out the twenty minutes that remained before the drawing of stumps, had succumbed to a combination of fading light and one of Hirst's swervers in the last over on Friday, the Gentlemen, with five wickets in hand, were faced with the task of notching two hundred and four runs in order to secure the victory. At lunchtime the position seemed hopeless. Two hundred and four is not a large score as scores go nowadays; but against this had to be placed the fact that Batkins, the Sussex professional, who had been drafted into the team at the eleventh hour, was scoring the proverbial success which attends eleventh-hour choices. From the press box, indeed, his bowling during the half-dozen overs before lunch appeared literally unplayable. The ball with which he dismissed MacLaren must have come back three inches. The wicket, too, was giving him just that assistance which a fast bowler needs, and he would have been a courageous man who would have asserted that the Gentlemen might even yet make a game of it. Immediately upon the re-start, however, the fortunes of the game veered completely round. Batkins' deliveries were wild and inaccurate, and the two batsmen, Riddell and James Douglas, speedily took advantage of this slice of luck. So much at home did they become that, scoring at a rapid rate, they remained together till the match was won, the Oxonian making the winning hit shortly before a quarter to six. The crowd, which was one of the largest we have ever seen at a Gentlemen *v.* Players match, cheered this wonderful performance to the echo. Douglas, the alteration in whose scholastic duties enabled him for the first time to turn out for the Gentlemen, made a number of lovely strokes in the course of his eighty-one. But even his performance was eclipsed by Riddell's great century. Without giving the semblance of a chance, he hit freely all round the wicket, two huge straight drives off successive balls from Batkins landing among the members' seats. When next our cousins from "down under" pay us a visit, we shall be surprised if Riddell does not show them . . .'

The rest is all about what Bill will do when he plays against Australia. Riddell is Bill. He is Aunt Edith's son. He is at New College, Oxford. Father says he is the best bat Oxford have had since he was up. But if you had seen him at lunch that day, you would never have dreamed of his making a century, or even double figures.

If you read what I wrote once about a thing that happened at our cricket week, you will remember who Batkins is. He came down to play for Sir Edward Cave's place against Much Middleford last year, and got everybody out except father, who made forty-nine not out. And he didn't get father out because I got my maid Saunders, whom he was in love with, to get him to bowl easy to father so that he could make fifty. He didn't make fifty, because the last man got out before he could; but it was all right. Anyhow, that's who Batkins was.

Perhaps you think that I tried the same thing again, and got Saunders to ask him to bowl easy to my cousin Bill in the Gentlemen v. Players match. But I didn't. I don't suppose he would have bowled badly in a big match like that for anyone, even Saunders. Besides, he and Saunders weren't on speaking terms at the time.

And that's really how the whole thing happened.

I really came into the story one night just before I was going to bed. Saunders was doing my hair. I was rather sleepy, and I was half dozing, when suddenly I heard a sort of curious sound behind me – a kind of mixture of a sniff and a gulp. I looked in the glass, and there was the reflection of Saunders with a sort of stuffed look about the face. Just then she looked up, and our eyes met in the glass. Hers were all reddy.

I said: 'Saunders!'

'Yes, miss.'

'What's the matter?'

'Matter, miss? Nothing, miss.'

'Why are you crying?'

She stiffened up and tried to look dignified. I wish she hadn't because she was holding a good deal of my hair at the time, and she pulled it – hard.

'Crying, miss! I wouldn't demean myself – no, I wouldn't.'

So I didn't say anything more for a bit, and she went on brushing my hair.

After about half a minute there was another gulp. I turned round.

'Look here, Saunders,' I said, 'you might as well tell me. You'll hurt yourself if you don't. What *is* up?'

(Because Saunders had always looked after me, long before I had my hair up – when I had it right down, not even tied half-way with a black ribbon. So we were rather friends.)

'You might say. I won't tell a soul.'

Then there was rather a ghark. A ghark is anything that makes you feel horrid and uncomfortable. It was a word invented by some girls I know, the Moncktons, and it supplied a long-felt want. It is a ghark if you ask somebody how somebody else is, and it turns out that they hate them or that they're dead. If you hurt anybody's feelings by accident, it is a ghark. This was one, because Saunders suddenly gave up all attempt at keeping it in, and absolutely howled. I sat there, not knowing what to do, and feeling wretched.

After a bit she got better, and then she told me what was the matter. She had had a quarrel with Mr Batkins, and all was over, and he had gone off, and she had not seen him since.

'I didn't know, miss, he'd take on so about me talking to Mr Harry Biggs when we met in the village. But he says: "Ellen," he says, "I must ask you to choose between that" – then he called him names, miss – "and me." "William," I says to him, "I won't 'ave such language from no man, I won't," I says, "not even if he is my fiancé," I says. So he says: "Promise me you won't speak to him again." So I says: "I won't, and don't you expect it." "Won't what?" he says, "won't speak?" "No," I says, "won't promise." "Ho!" he says, "so this is the end, is it? All's over, is it?" So I says: "Yes, William Batkins," I says, "all is over; and here's your ring what you gave me, and the photograph of yourself in a locket. And very ugly it is," I says; "and don't you come 'anging round me again," I says. And so he rushed out and never came back.'

She broke down once more at the thought of it.

This was the worst ghark I had ever had; because I couldn't think how I could make the thing better.

'Why don't you write to him?' I asked.

'I wouldn't demean myself, miss. And I don't know his address.'

'He plays for a county, so I suppose a letter addressed care of the county ground would reach him. I remember being told which county, but I've forgotten it. Do you know?'

'No, miss. He told me it was a first-class one, but I don't remember which it was.'

'Well, I'll look at the paper tomorrow, and see. He is sure to be playing.'

But though I looked all through the cricket page, I could not find him.

That was Wednesday. On Thursday, my brother Bob arrived from London, bringing with him a friend of his, a Mr Townend, who said he was an artist, but I had never seen any of his pictures. He explained this at dinner. He said that he spent the winter thinking out schemes for big canvases, and in the summer he was too busy playing cricket to be able to get to work on them.

'I say, we've been up at Lord's today,' he said. He was a long, pleasant-looking young man, with a large smile and unbrushed hair. 'Good game, rather. Er – um – Gentlemen'll have all their work cut out to win, I think.'

'Ah!' said father. 'Gentlemen v. Players, eh? My young nephew Willie is playing. Been doing well for Oxford this season – W.B. Riddell.'

'Oh, I say, really? Good field. Players batted first. Fiery wicket, but it'll wear well, I think. Er – um – Johnny Knox was making them get up at the nursery end rather, but Tyldesley seems to be managing 'em all right. Made fifty when we left. Looked like stopping. By the way, friend of yours was playing for the pros – Billy Batkins, the Sussex man. Bob was telling me that you knocked the cover off him down here last summer.'

Father beamed.

'Oh!' he said. 'Good deal of luck in it, of course. I managed to make a few.'

'Forty-nine not out,' I said, 'and a splendid innings, too.'

'Oh, I say, really?' said Mr Townend, stretching out a long, thin hand in the direction of the strawberries. 'Takes some doing, that. You know, they only put him into the team at the last moment. But if anyone's going to win the match for them, it'll be he. Just suit him, the wicket ought to, on the last day.'

'Regular Day of Judgment for the Gentlemen,' said Bob. 'Somebody ought to run up to town and hold Bill's hand while he bats, to encourage him.'

I said: 'Father, mayn't I go up to London tomorrow? You know Aunt Edith said only the other day that she wished you would let me. And I *should* like to see Bill bat.'

Father looked disturbed. Any sudden proposal confuses him. And I could see that he was afraid that if I went, he might have to go too. And he hates London.

I didn't say anything more just then; but after dinner, when Bob and Mr Townend were playing billiards, I went to his study and asked him again.

'I should love to go,' I said, sitting on the arm of his chair. 'There's really no need for you to come, if you don't want to. Saunders could go with me.'

'It's uncommonly short notice for your aunt, my dear,' said father doubtfully.

'*She* won't mind. She's always got tons of room. And she said come whenever I liked. And Bill would be awfully pleased, wouldn't he?'

'Only make him nervous.'

I said: 'Oh, no. He'd like it. Well, may I?'

I kissed father on the top of the head, and he said I might.

So next day up I went with Saunders, feeling like a successful general.

I got there just before dinner. I found my cousin Bill rather depressed. He had come back from Lord's, where the Gentlemen had been getting the worst of it. The Players had made three hundred and thirty something, and the Gentlemen had made two hundred and twenty-three. Then the Players had gone in again and made two hundred and six, which wasn't good, Bill said, but left the Gentlemen more than three hundred behind.

'And we lost one wicket tonight,' he said, 'for nine; and the pitch is getting beastly. We shall never make the runs.'

'How many did you make, Bill?'

'Ten. Run out. And I particularly wanted to get a few. Just like my luck.'

I asked Aunt Edith afterwards why Bill had been so keen on making runs in this match more than any other, and she said it was because it was the biggest match he had ever played in. But Bill told me the real reason before breakfast the next morning. He was engaged, and *she* had come to watch him play.

'And I made a measly ten!' said Bill. 'If I don't do something this innings, I shall never be able to look her in the face again. And I know she thinks a lot of my batting. She told me so. It's probably been an eye-opener for her.'

'Poor old Bill!' I said. 'Perhaps you'll do better today.'

'I feel as if I should never make a run again,' he said.

But he did.

I thought it all over that night. Of course, the difficult part was how to let Mr Batkins know that Saunders wanted everything to be forgiven and forgotten. Because he would be out in the field all the time.

I said to Bill: 'You'll be seeing Mr Batkins, the bowler, tomorrow, won't you?'

He said: 'Yes, worse luck, I shall.'

'Then, look here, Bill,' I said, 'will you do me a favour? I want to speak to him particularly. Can I, do you think? Can you make him come and talk to me?'

'You can take a man from the pavilion,' said Bill, 'but you can't make him talk. What do you want him for?'

'It's private.'

'You're not after his autograph, are you?'

'Of course I'm not. Why should I want his autograph?'

'Some kids would give their eyes for it. They shoot in picture-postcards to all the leading pros, and make them sign 'em.'

I said nothing, but I did not like Bill hinting that I was a kid; because I'm not. I've had my hair up more than a year now.

I said: 'Well, I don't, anyhow. I simply want to speak to him.'

'Shy bird, Batkins. Probably if he hears that there's a lady waiting to see him, he'll lock himself in the changing-room and refuse to come out. Still, I'll have a try. During the lunch interval would be best – just before they go on to the field.'

Then I arranged it with Saunders.

I said: 'I shall be seeing Mr Batkins tomorrow, Saunders. If you like, I'll give him a note from you, and wait for an answer.'

'Oh, miss!' said Saunders.

'Then you can say what you like about wanting to make it up, without the ghark of doing it to his face. And if it's all right, which it's certain to be, I'll tell him to come round to Sloane Street after the match, and have some supper, and it'll all be ripping. I'm sure Aunt Edith won't mind.'

Then there was another ghark. Saunders broke down again and got quite hysterical, and said I was too good to her, and she wouldn't demean herself, and she didn't know what to write, and she was sure she would never speak to him again, were it ever so, and she'd go and get the note ready now, and heaps of other things. And when she was better, she went downstairs to write to Mr Batkins.

I believe she found it very difficult to make up the letter, because I didn't see her again that night, and she only gave it to me when we came home for lunch next day. We had decided to take Bill home in the motor to lunch, unless he had gone in in the morning and was not out, when he wouldn't have time.

We sat in the seats to the right of the pavilion. The girl Bill was engaged to was there, with her mother, and I was introduced to her. She was very anxious that Bill should make lots of runs. She was a very nice girl. I only wished I could use my influence with Mr Batkins, as I had done before, to make him bowl badly. But he did just the opposite. They put him on after about half an hour, and everybody said he was bowling splendidly. It got rather dull, because the batsmen didn't seem able to make any runs, and they wouldn't hit out. I thought our matches at home were much more interesting. Everybody tries to hit there.

Bill was in the pavilion all the morning; but when the umpires took the bails off, he came out to us, and we all went back in the motor. Bill was more gloomy than I had ever seen him.

'It's a little hard,' he said. 'Just when Hirst happens to have an off-day – he was bowling tosh this morning – and the wicket doesn't suit Rhodes, and one thinks one really has got a chance of taking a few, this man Batkins starts and bowls about fifty per cent above his proper form. Did you see that ball that got MacLaren? It was the sort of beastly thing you get in nightmares. Fast as an express and coming in half a foot. If Batkins doesn't get off his length after lunch, we're cooked. And he's a teetotaller, too!'

I tried to cheer him up by talking about the girl he was engaged to, but it only made him worse.

'And it's in front of a girl like that,' he said, 'who believes in a chap, too, mind you, that I'm probably going to make a beastly exhibition of myself. That ball of Billy Batkins'll get me five times out of six. And the sixth time, too.'

Saunders gave me the letter as I was going out. I reminded Bill that he had promised to get hold of Mr Batkins for me.

'I'd forgotten,' he said. 'All right. When we get to the ground, come along with me.'

So we left Aunt Edith in the covered seats and walked round to behind the pavilion.

'Wait here a second,' said Bill. 'I'll send him out. You'll have to hurry up with whatever you're going to say to him, because the Players will be taking the field in about three minutes.'

I waited there, prodding the asphalt with my parasol, and presently Mr Batkins appeared, blushing violently and looking very embarrassed.

'Did you want to see me, miss?' he said. I said 'Yes,' feeling rather gharked and not knowing how to begin.

'You're Mr Batkins, aren't you?' I said at last. It was rather silly, because he couldn't very well be anybody else.

'You played against us last summer,' I said, 'for Sir Edward Cave, at Much Middlefold.'

He started. I suppose the name made him think of Saunders.

The bell began ringing in the pavilion. He shuffled his feet. The spikes made a horrid noise on the asphalt, like a squeaking slate-pencil.

'Was there anything?' he said. 'I shall have

to be going out in a minute to bowl.' He pronounced it as if it rhymed with 'fowl'.

So I saw there was no time to waste, and I plunged straight into the thing.

I said: 'You know Saunders doesn't *really* care a bit for Mr Harry Biggs. She told me so.'

He turned crimson. He had been rather red before, but nothing to this.

'Me and Ellen, miss –' he began.

'Oh, I know,' I said. 'She has told me all about it. She's awfully miserable, Mr Batkins. And she would have written long before, to make it up, only she didn't know your address. I've got a letter from her here, which –'

He simply grabbed the letter and tore it open. I wish I knew what was in it. He read it again and again, breathing very hard, and really looking almost as if he were going to cry.

'Can I tell Saunders it's all right?' I said.

He wouldn't answer for an age. He kept on reading the letter. Then he said: 'Oh, yes, miss,' very fervently. He was what Bob calls 'absolutely rattled.' I suppose he must have been fretting awfully all the time, really, only he wouldn't write and tell Saunders so, but let concealment, like a worm i' the bud, feed on his damask cheek.

(I used to know the whole bit once, to say by heart. I learned it when I did lessons, before I put my hair up. But I've forgotten all but that one piece now.)

'And you'll come to supper tonight? You've got the address on the letter. It's on the right-hand side of Sloane Street, as you go down.'

'Oh, yes, miss. Thank you, miss.'

And off he dashed in a great hurry,

because the Players were just going out into the field.

So that's why 'Batkins' deliveries were wild and inaccurate' after lunch. Poor man, he was so flurried by the whole thing that he could hardly bowl at all. The bowler at the other end got a man caught in his first over, and then Bill went in. And Bill hit him in all directions. It was a lovely innings. I don't think I ever enjoyed one more – not even father's forty-nine not out against the Cave men. They took poor Mr Batkins off after a time, but Bill was set by then, and they couldn't get him out. He went on and on, till at last he got his century and won the match. And everybody rushed across the ground from the cheap seats, and stood by the pavilion railings, yelling. And Bill had to lean out of a window and bow.

'I withdraw what I said about friend Batkins being a teetotaller,' said Bill after dinner that night to me. 'No man could have bowled as rottenly as he did after lunch, on lemonade. It was the sort of stuff you get in a village game ' very fast and beautifully inaccurate.'

Then I told him how it had happened, and he owned that his suspicions were unjust. We were in the drawing-room at the time. The drawing-room is just over the kitchen. Bill stretched out his hands, palms downwards, and looked at the floor.

'Bless you, my children!' he said.

Bill is really an awfully good sort. When I was leaving Aunt Edith's, he came up and gave me a mysterious little paper parcel. I opened it, and inside it was a jeweller's cardboard box. And inside that, in cotton wool, was the duckiest little golden bat.

'A presentation bat,' he explained, 'because you made a century for Gentlemen *v*. Players.'

Between the Innings

It seemed to be the general opinion that the country wanted rain. Meaning by the country the half-dozen of us who were gathered together in the billiard-room at Heath Hall smoking, playing pool, and talking cricket 'shop', with particular reference to the match which would come to an end on the following day.

It was, indeed, a most solemn and important occasion. This was the last night but one of the Hall cricket-week, and, so far, success had crowned the efforts of the Hall team as never before.

The Zingari had come and gone, routed – a five-wickets affair. The Band of Brothers had headed us on the first innings, but failed in the next, and we had come through for the second time with half our wickets in hand. We were now in the middle of the Incogniti match, and our one aim in life was to win this and set up a Hall week record. Never before had the Hall been able to score more than a couple of victories in the three matches.

The best week up to the present had occurred six years before, when Ronald Heath was captain of the Oxford team, and Jack Heath half-way up the list of the same. Then we had won two and drawn the third favourably.

What made this season's week such a triumph was the fact that, on paper, we were not so strong as usual. Jack was in India playing polo instead of cricket, and Ronald was obliged to confine his efforts to umpiring, having strained a muscle in a county match of the previous week. We should have missed them more had it not been for the unusually fine form in which young Tommy Heath, the third of the brothers, happened to find himself at this crisis.

Tommy had captained Winchester that season and scored a century against Eton; but even that had not prepared us for his feats during this week. He had followed up two brilliant innings in the earlier games with a masterly eighty-four in the match now in progress, which match was now in such a position that it might be said to be anybody's game. We had batted first. Wicket hard and true.

The Hall ground is small, and scoring is generally fast there. Starting at a quarter to eleven, we had made two hundred and ten by lunch-time for six wickets. By three o'clock we were all out for two hundred and fifty.

It was not a large score for the ground. Having lived all my life at my father's rectory across the Park, I could remember many Hall weeks, including at least three when the side that had won the toss had nearly succeeded in putting four hundred on the board before going the way of all batting sides. But two hundred and fifty proved good enough in the present case. The Incogs had replied with two hundred and twenty-three. In an hour and a half of the second innings we had put up a hundred and thirty for seven wickets by the time stumps were drawn for the day.

Wherefore we prayed for rain. A steady downpour in the night, and the wicket would play easy for the first hour on the morrow, during which period our last three men might be expected to put on at least another fifty. Which, if the sun came out, as it probably would, ought to be enough, we thought, to give us a winning lead.

Dalgliesh flung up the window and peered earnestly out into the night.

'It looks like rain,' he said. 'There's thunder hanging about somewhere.'

'Yellow to play,' said Felstone, moving round the table after chalking his cue – 'dot vos me. No good. I don't think pool's my *forte*. Hullo! Lightning.'

He joined Dalgliesh at the window. Summer lightning flickered across the dark opening. It was oppressively hot. Too hot to last. The rain was bound to come soon. But it might delay its advent for another twenty-four hours, by which time, like most late-comers in this world, it would find its services not required and even unpopular.

'Give us three hours' good, steady, soaking downpour,' said Dalgliesh meditatively, 'and we shall have those Incogs by the short hairs. We shall then call upon our Mr Peter Baynes to give his celebrated imitation of Braund.'

'On a nice, sticky pitch,' I replied, being the Peter Baynes alluded to and the slow bowler of the Hall team, 'with a hot sun drying it up while you look at it, I'll see what I can do for you. But if the wicket's going to be the mixture of concrete and granite it was this afternoon, gallery performances are off and I shall take to golf.'

For the Hall ground on a day such as we had just had was enough to break the heart of any slow bowler, who likes assistance from the pitch when he embarks upon his duties. The combination of good wicket and short boundaries had done neither myself nor my analysis any good that afternoon.

'Did your father read the prayer for rain last Sunday?' asked Melhuish in his solemn way.

'Yes,' I said, 'he did.'

'Good!' said Melhuish. 'We shall need it.'

The door opened as he spoke, and Wentworth Flood came in. Flood was a man I cordially disliked, and I have reason to believe that my feelings were shared by at least a good working majority of those present. How he came to be tame cat in a house the very atmosphere of which breathed sport, I had never been able to understand. I take it, however, that women, however many sons they may have playing in first-class cricket, and however interested they may be in the game, cherish a secret liking for a man who can always be relied on to make himself useful in the drawing-room instead of seeking his pleasure out-of-doors.

Wentworth Flood dressed well, looked neat, never broke things, handled tea-cups admirably, played a number of card-games with more than average skill, acted if there were theatricals, and was always ready to play an accompaniment on the mandoline; so, I suppose, Lady Heath saw reasons for having him about the house which we did not.

He was a small man, with an almost irritating lack of anything wrong in his personal appearance. His hair was parted exactly in the middle. His tie was tied with a nicety which almost suggested the made-up article. His voice was 'ever soft, gentle, and low,' which, though it may be an 'excellent thing in a woman,' is not such an endearing quality in man.

'Been playing bridge, Flood?' asked Dalgliesh, breaking one of those awkward pauses which occur when the uncongenial spirit breaks in upon the social gathering.

'No,' said Flood precisely. 'I have not been playing bridge. I have been playing the mandoline.'

There did not seem much that could be said by way of comment on this. Somehow the mention of mandolines in the middle of the profound and serious discussion of a cricket match struck us as almost blasphemous. Dalgliesh snorted, and Manners, whose turn it was to play, nearly cut the cloth. Otherwise there was no attempt at criticism.

'Tommy Heath tells me we shall win the cricket match tomorrow,' said Flood, after a silence lasting for the space of two strokes of the cue.

'So we shall,' said Dalgliesh, 'if it rains.'

'But I thought you could not play cricket in the rain?'

'No, but rain occasionally stops, and then the wicket gets soft,' said Manners.

'And then Baynes leaves off those half-volleys which worry Sir John's nesting pheasants,' said Dalgliesh, 'and gets some work on the ball.'

'But why should it matter if the ground is soft?' inquired Flood.

'Because,' I said, 'a merciful Providence, watching over slow bowlers, has ordained that batsmen make fewer runs on a soft pitch, and get out quicker. That's why.'

Flood looked thoughtful, and I noticed that he went to the window, and stood for some time gazing at the sky. At the moment I wondered why, and what possible interest he could take in the weather. A drawing-room is just as pleasant on a wet as on a dry day.

It was at eleven o'clock, when I left the billiard-room to begin my homeward journey, that I found out his reason. In the hall I met Tommy Heath. He looked worried and rather pale.

'Going already?' he said. 'It's quite early. Come for a bit of a stroll with me first. I've got something I want to tell you.'

We walked slowly round to the back of the house, and came to an anchor on a garden-seat that stood against the wall, facing the Park.

'Well?' I said.

Tommy and I had been to different schools, and I was some years his senior, but we had known one another since his sailor-suit days; and we generally told each other things.

Tommy lit a cigarette, an act which would possibly have disturbed his headmaster if he had seen it.

'I'm in rather a hole,' he said.

'What's up now?' I asked.

'It's that man Flood. Hope he's not a friend

of yours, by the way?'

'Not in the very least,' I said. 'Don't let that worry you. What has Flood been doing to you?'

'Well, it was like this. He'd been trying to be funny the whole evening, and then he started shooting off his confounded epigrams about cricket. I'm hanged if I can remember how it all came about, but we met on the stairs, going to the drawing-room, and he began chipping the Hall team. Beastly bad form, considering I was captain. I couldn't think of anything much to say, don't you know, but I had to say something, so I said: "Well, I bet you ten to one the Hall wins tomorrow, whatever you think of the team."'

'What happened then? That wouldn't squash him.'

'It didn't,' said Tommy briefly. 'The man took me up like a shot. "Ten to one?" he said. I believe he's a Jew. He looked just like one. "Ten to one? In what? Shall we say fivers?"'

I sat up.

'You don't mean to say you were idiot enough to make it fivers?' I said.

'Not so loud, man,' said Tommy, 'I don't want everyone to hear. Yes, I was. I don't know why I did it. I must have been cracked. But, somehow, looking at him standing there, and knowing that I should feel scored off if I backed out, I said, yes, fivers if he liked. Do you know, the man actually planked it down in a beastly little pocket-book, and asked me to initial it. So, there you are. That's the situation. And if we don't win tomorrow I'm in for rather a pleasant thing.'

'But, Tommy,' I gasped, 'this is absurd!

You haven't got fifty pounds in the world. Suppose we lose tomorrow? And we probably shall if it don't rain tonight. What will you do?'

'Oh, it's simple enough. I shall go to the governor. I've got a couple of hundred quid in the bank, but I can't draw without his leave. He'll want to know why I'm asking for a big sum like that. I shall tell him it's for a bet.'

'And then what?' I said.

'And then he'll give me the fifty pounds, and not let me go to the 'Varsity. Ever since he had to pay up for Ronald's Oxford debts – he ran them up a bit, as you probably remember – he's told us plainly that the first sign we show of not being able to take care of money scratches us as far as the 'Varsity's concerned. Jack had to be awfully careful when he went up. That's what'll happen.'

I was silent. I knew that he had set his heart on going up to Oxford and adding a third to the family list of cricket Blues. And I knew that Sir John, rigid as steel in matters of this sort, would keep his word.

'You can't back out?' I said at length. 'Flood surely must know that ten to one was simply a way of speaking. He can't imagine that you were really offering him odds.'

'Of course he didn't,' said Tommy bitterly. 'Flood's not a fool. He's the other thing. But, all the same, I can't get out of it now. I'm not going to give a man like Flood the whip-hand of me, even if I lose my chance of a Blue through it. There's only one way out. We must win tomorrow.'

'I wish we could water that wicket,' I said. 'If only that infernal concrete turf would get a soaking I could make the ball do a bit. As it is, I'm helpless.'

I made my way across the Park in a very gloomy frame of mind. It was warmer than ever. The sky was inky black, except when a flash of summer lightning lit it up. I knew every inch of the Park, or I might not have been able to find my way.

My nearest path lay across the cricket-field. When I got to the pitch where we had been playing that afternoon I stopped. But for the white creases, which showed faintly through the darkness, I should have passed by without seeing it. I stooped, and pressed a finger into the turf. It was dry as tinder. On such a wicket, with a whole day in which to make the runs, the Incogniti could hardly help winning, even if our tail were to wag more energetically than the most sanguine among us hoped.

Poor Tommy's chances of a Blue seemed small. Somehow, perhaps on account of the excitement of the day or the electricity with which the thunder-clouds filled the air, I felt disinclined for bed. The church clock struck half-past eleven. I sat down by the side of the pitch and lit my pipe. It was pleasant, if a little eerie, out there in the middle of the Park. I sat on where I was long after my pipe had gone out, listening dreamily to the thousand and one faint noises of a summer night.

I think I must have been falling asleep, when suddenly a new sound came to my ears, and I was broad awake in a moment. It was none of those thousand and one noises which are all unaccountable yet not startling. It was the soft tread of a human foot on the turf, and a heavy breathing, as of one working hard. I could just see a dim figure coming slowly towards me. A few yards away it halted, and I heard a thud, as it set down its burden on the ground.

It was the noise that followed the thud that made me dart forward so rapidly. It was the unmistakable sloppy splash of water forced out of the spout of a can. I realised the situation at once. Somebody had come to water the wicket.

I am glad to say that I abandoned the notion that it was Tommy a clear three seconds before I became aware of the criminal's real identity. I felt instinctively that it would take a deal more than the thought of his bet to make him sink to such depths.

'Oh!' gasped a frightened voice. 'Who's that?'

I recognised the voice. The intruder was the youngest of the four Heaths; Tommy's sister Ella.

'Ella!' I cried. 'What on earth – ?'

I heard her draw a long breath of relief.

'Oh, is that you, Peter? How you frightened me!'

'What are you doing out here at this time of night?'

'It was so hot, I couldn't sleep. I –'

'And what is that can for?' I inquired coolly.

'I don't care!' she said defiantly. 'I meant to do it, and I would have done it if you hadn't caught me. Don't glare at me like that, Peter. I don't care a bit. I heard every word you and poor old Tommy were saying. You didn't know my bedroom window was over that seat.

I heard you say that you wished you could water the pitch. It's no use looking shocked, Peter, because I'm not sorry. Not a bit.'

The main points of the affair had found their way to my understanding by now. I was conscious of a curious, dazed feeling. It was like a vivid dream.

'But, Ella,' I said at last, 'it's impossible. You can't have understood. Don't you see what a frightful thing – It isn't as if you knew nothing about cricket. You know as well as I do what it means to doctor the pitch between the innings.'

'I don't care!' she repeated. 'I would do anything to save Tommy from that *beast*, Mr Flood.'

'As if Tommy wouldn't rather lose his Blue a hundred times sooner than be saved like that.'

There was a pause.

'Peter.'

'Well?'

'You know – you know you said you'd do anything for me?'

I may state here – briefly – that, like the great majority of the youth of the neighbour-hood, I was head over ears in love with Tommy's sister Ella. The occasion to which she referred had been a painful one for me. We had been sitting out the eighth waltz in the conservatory on the night of the Hunt Ball. To put the thing in a nutshell, I had proposed with all the clumsy energy of an enthusiastic novice, and had been rejected.

'You know you did.'

I said nothing.

There was a very long pause.

'Peter!' said a still small voice.

'Yes?' I said.

'Don't you think – just *one* canful?'

I am ashamed to say that for a single moment I wavered. I verily believe that Mr Apted of the Oval would have thought seriously about ruining one of his masterpieces if the request had come to him in such a form. But I rallied myself.

'Let me just sketch for you,' I said, in the calm, dispassionate voice of a professor lecturing on osteology or some kindred subject, 'what would be the result of that canful. We should probably win the match. Tommy would win his bet, and go to Oxford. Every single man in the Incogniti team would see that the wicket had been tampered with, and every single man would be too polite to say a word about it. But, little by little the story would get about, and after that I should imagine that the teams which come here during the Hall week would have previous engagements for a few years. When Tommy went away to play in matches, people would ask one another if he was one of the Heaths of that place where they water the wicket when it suits their fancy. And then –'

'Peter, stop!'

I stopped.

'Would you mind carrying that can to the stable-yard, please?'

I took up the can.

'Good-night!' I said.

'Come back. Listen! I – I'm very grateful to you, Peter. You've saved me from disgracing the family. I'm very, *very* grateful to you!'

I murmured inarticulately. Then I started,

for something wet had fallen upon my hand. From every side came a faint patter, growing in volume with each succeeding second. A warm rivulet trickled between my collar and my neck.

'By George! I cried, 'here's the rain!'

And, indeed, the downpour had begun in earnest. We were standing in a vast shower-bath.

'You must go in at once!' I said. 'You'll be catching cold.'

'Peter!'

I stopped.

'You *will* bowl your best tomorrow, won't you?'

'That is my present intention,' I said.

There was a pause, broken by the swishing of the rain on to the turf.

'Peter, I – you know – sometimes – I don't always say what – what I mean.'

Another pause.

'If you save Tommy tomorrow, I'll –'

'Will you?' I said eagerly.

'I'll see,' said Ella, and vanished into the darkness in the direction of the Hall.

At three-fifty on the following afternoon Mr Wentworth Flood lost five pounds, which annoyed him. At precisely the same moment I won something of a greater value, which pleased me very much.

On Fast Bowling –
by 'N.A. Knox'

(ghosted by Wodehouse and reproduced in
the *Daily Mail* 17 May 1907)

It is a very difficult thing to give advice on how
to become a fast bowler. Pace is to a great
extent a gift, like red hair, or collecting
postage-stamps.

No man by thought can add a cubit to his
stature, and that is just the difficulty, for it is
height as much as anything that makes a man
a fast bowler. Batting can be acquired (personally, I have never done it, and am never
likely to), but a fast bowler, like Topsy, 'just
grows'. Lack of height is no drawback in a
batsman, witness Abel and Tyldesley. But in a
bowler who wishes to cultivate speed, it is a
very serious drawback. I can imagine Little
Tich, if he gave his massive mind to the business, becoming a stylish and effective batsman; but I do not see the wicketkeeper
retreating a dozen yards, or the batsman leap-
ing nimbly away to square leg if he began to
bowl.

Height is not everything, of course. Fielder
and Cotter seem to get on very well without it.
But it is half the battle. I might have headed
this article, 'For tall men only'. We will
assume, therefore that the wouldbe fast
bowler is a man of inches. One of the worst
pitfalls which will lie in his path is the tempta-

tion to over-bowl himself when he is a boy. It is a strong temptation. At school, pace is such a very valuable asset. Sheer speed is enough to account for the average school batsman who is not in the first eleven. Wickets in minor matches at a public school are normally of a bumpy and corrugated nature, and a reputation for being able to 'plug them down' is worth six wickets an innings to a boy.

In these circumstances, he is scarcely to be expected to refrain from sacrificing everything to pace. But if he is wise, he will not do it. The momentary pleasure is great, but it is not a good preparation. One knows of scores of cases where promising fast bowlers have bowled themselves out at school. This is particularly so when they play in important cricket at an early age. The average school captain is not likely to spare a bowler who can get wickets against another school, however bad it may be for his future to toil away while his strength is undeveloped. The first year I was in the Dulwich team, I only bowled thirty-three overs. I did not like it then, but I am glad of it now.

Another danger is that the fast bowler when at school will devote himself to pace at the expense of spin and break. This is fatal. On modern first-class wickets, one must get some spin and break if the ball is to beat the bat. At school fast, straight bowling will always get wickets. Unless the habit of breaking has been acquired gradually and thoroughly, a bowler cannot succeed in first class cricket. I would advise the man with aspirations towards pace to bowl fast medium, except in actual matches, and to concentrate his whole attention on length and spin. Accuracy is just as important for a fast bowler as for a slow. A poor batsman will frequently be 'outed' by a half-volley, if it is speedy enough, but it is not often that one catches a county cricketer off his guard. A fast bowler who loses his length is a gift to any good batsman.

Height makes for pace in a bowler, but still more so does looseness of limb. To keep his shoulder loose is the first duty of the man of pace. Mere strength is often a drawback. It is an excellent trait in a man to be able to lift big dumb-bells with his right hand, but if he means to go through a first-class season, he would do well to choose some other form of amusement for his spare time. Personally, I never use dumb-bells or anything of the kind. In the winter, I play golf whenever I can. I play for pleasure and not with any idea of training for the cricket season, but I play left-handed, and my right shoulder consequently comes in for a good deal of exercise. I should imagine that boxing was a very fine form of exercise for a bowler, but I have never tried it.

Lastly, to my mind the chief quality necessary for the man who wishes to succeed as a fast bowler is a certain mental energy. Fast bowling may be scientific, or it may be merely brutal – to judge from some of the letters I saw in the papers last summer, I should think a good many people took the latter view – but, whatever it is, it is not a restful occupation. If the doctor ordered me a complete rest, I should not go out in a hot sun and bowl my fastest on a true wicket to Tom Hayward or Hirst. It is real work all the time. I am particularly unfortunate in finding it necessary to take such a long run. (Even this, however, has its consolations. On some grounds, I inevitably cause the crowd to roar with laughter by this simple method; and it is good to feel that one is amusing people.)

It is a very severe strain to keep up one's pace, even on a cool day. But a hot day is the real test. Last summer was anything but a treat for fast bowlers. There are days when The Oval turf seems like concrete, and when it is is like bowling in an oven. The last day of Surrey and Middlesex at The Oval was one of them. It was the sort of day one would have liked to spend in a hammock or on the river. At the end of half a dozen overs I felt that I would like to sacrifice everything in the world for an iced drink. At such a time it is only by the exercise of much willpower that one can force oneself to bowl really fast. To drop into fast-medium would be such a relief. It is a struggle to fight down the temptation. But unless you can do it, you cannot be a really good fast bowler.

The word 'trier' has been overdone by writers on cricket, but really it is the only word which adequately describes the good player. Walter Lees, to my mind, is the model trier. He puts his heart into every ball, and lets himself go as cheerfully when catches are being dropped off him, as he does when everything comes off right for him.

I began my remarks on the determination and keenness which go to make the good fast bowler with the word 'Lastly'; but I shall have to imitate the curate and follow my 'Lastly' with 'But one word more'. Too much stress cannot be laid on the value to any bowler, and to a fast bowler more than all, of an equable temper. To lose one's temper under strain of adverse circumstances is bad at any game, but worst at cricket. A bowler who does so when his catches are not being held has every possible excuse. But he does not want excuses. He wants wickets. And the way to get them is to keep an unruffled mind. It is maddening when you have been tempting a batsman to 'touch' one in the slips at the expense of several boundaries, to see that catch laid gently on the floor by one of the slips. It is also annoying when an obviously beaten batsman snicks your best off his wicket to the boundary, or when an appeal for an obvious lbw is given against you, though, in the last case, you have the small satisfaction of feeling that the batsman is not altogether happy either.

But all these things must be borne with fortitude. A fast bowler must be a machine. His run, if it is not to wear him out in a few overs, must be as regular and mechanical as possible, always the same number of strides, and his mind must work like a machine does. He must be above disappointment at any bad luck he may have. If county bowlers did not train themselves into this frame of mind, they would become grey-headed in a couple of seasons. '*Aequam memento rebus in arduis*' should be the motto of every fast bowler, or, to translate freely, 'Buck up, and never mind what happens'.

As to lunch, in conclusion. A dangerous meal, lunch. I have known men bowl like angels before it, and roll on to the field like gorged pythons afterwards. One wants enough to keep up one's strength, but not too much. Avoid whisky. For half an hour after it, one feels like working miracles. After that half-hour, what one wants is a miracle to enable one to feel like working. Dry ginger ale is the best lunch-drink in my opinion. It quenches the thirst and has no bad effects. I might advertise a certain brand which I always drink during matches, but I will refrain.

(Ten weeks later Knox made his debut for England at Headingley. He was called on to bowl only three overs, taking one wicket; South Africa were dismissed for 110 and 75 with Colin Blythe taking 15/99, England winning by 53 runs. And ironically given Knox's complaints about bowling on hot days, this match was badly affected by rain).

Missed!

The sun in the heavens was beaming;
The breeze bore an odour of hay,
My flannels were spotless and gleaming,
My heart was unclouded and gay;
The ladies, all gaily apparelled,
Sat round looking on at the match,
In the tree-tops the dicky-birds carolled,
All was peace till I bungled that catch.

My attention the magic of summer
Had lured from the game – which was wrong;
The bee (that inveterate hummer)
Was droning its favourite song.
I was tenderly dreaming of Clara
(On her not a girl is a patch);
When, ah horror! there soared through the air a
Decidedly possible catch.

I heard in a stupor the bowler
Emit a self-satisfied 'Ah!'
The small boys who sat on the roller
Set up an expectant 'Hurrah!'
The batsman with grief from the wicket
Himself had begun to detach –
And I uttered a groan and turned sick – It
Was over. I'd buttered the catch.

Oh ne'er, if I live to a million,
Shall I feel such a terrible pang.
From the seats in the far-off pavilion
A loud yell of ecstasy rang.
By the handful my hair (which is auburn)
I tore with a wrench from my thatch,
And my heart was seared deep with a raw burn
At the thought that I'd foozled that catch.

Ah, the bowler's low querulous mutter,
Point's loud, unforgettable scoff!
Oh, give me my driver and putter!
Henceforward my game shall be golf.
If I'm asked to play cricket hereafter,
I am wholly determined to scratch.
Life's void of all pleasure and laughter;
I bungled the easiest catch.

The Cricketer in Winter

The days are growing short and cold;
Approaches Autumn, ay and chill Yule:
The latest bowler now has bowled
His latest devastating pillule.
Gone are the creases, gone the 'pegs';
The bungling fieldsman now no more errs
By letting balls go through his legs
And giving batsmen needless fourers.

Things of the past are drive and cut,
With which erstwhile we would astound men;
The gay pavilion's doors are shut;
The turf is given up to groundmen;
Gone is the beautiful length-ball,
Gone, too, the batsman who would snick it;
Silent his partner's cheery call.
Football usurps the place of cricket.

Now, as incessantly it pours,
And each succeeding day seems bleaker,
The cricketer remains indoors,
And quaffs mayhap the warming beaker.
Without, the scrummage heaves and slips;
Not his to play the muddied oaf. A
Well-seasoned pipe between his lips,
He reads his *Wisden* on the sofa.

Or, if in vein for gentle toil,
Before he seeks a well-earned pillow,
He takes a flask of linseed oil
And tends his much-enduring willow,
Feeling the while, what time he drops
The luscious fluid by degrees on,
Given half-volleys and long-hops,
How nobly it will drive next season!

Then to his couch, to dream till day
Of fifties when the pitch was sticky,
Of bowling crisply 'put away,'
Though it was manifestly tricky,
Of umpires, confident appeals,
Hot shots at point, mid-off, and cover,
Of cricket-lunches (perfect meals!):-
Such dreams attend the cricket-lover.

And, though the streets be deep in snow,
Though slippery pavements make him stumble,
Though rain descends, though blizzards blow,
It matters not: he scorns to grumble.
What if it lightens, thunders, hails,
And common men grow daily glummer,
In him contentment never fails;
To such a man it's always Summer.

The Umpire

I'm monarch of all I survey;
There isn't a ruler to-day,
Not a Sultan or Tsar
Of a country afar,
Who can boast of a similar sway.
There's always a something that checks them
No matter how great they may be.
They've got armies and such,
But their power's not much
If you only compare 'em with me.

For I'm the infallible umpire,
The strict, indispensable umpire.
And you've got to abide
By what I decide;
It isn't a matter for doubt.
If you're peer or you're peasant,
You've got to look pleasant
And go when I tell you you're out!
Out!
How's that? Run along, sir, you're out.

The swell from the swaggerest club,
The 'rabbit', who's there as a sub.,
The veteran grey
(Who was good in his day),
The wholly incompetent cub,
The man who thinks cricket a business,
And the fellow who thinks it a spree,

I handle the lot,
And I show 'em what's what;
They all knuckle under to me.

For I'm the inflexible umpire,
The stern, incorruptible umpire;
I add to the woes
Of the bowler who throws,
When 'No ball!' I incessantly shout.
And the batsmen pursue me
With looks that are gloomy,
When I beg to inform 'em they're out.
Out!
How's that? Run along, sir, you're out.

There once was a time when I played;
But those days won't return, I'm afraid,
For alas, I must own
That I reached eighteen stone
And a quarter when last I was weighed.
I was once good at saving the single,
My limbs were so lissom and free,
But when bulkiness came
I abandoned the game
As a little too active for me.

And now I am simply the umpire,
The massive and dignified umpire,
My eyes are as keen
As they ever have been,
For your sight doesn't fail though you're stout.
If you're leg before wicket,
Or caught when you snick it,
I see it, and tell you you're out.
Out!
How's that? Off you go, sir, you're out!

Waterstones

Unit 69
Eastgate Shopping Centre
Inverness
IV2 3PR
01463 233500
SALE TRANSACTION

VINTAGE CAPER, THE	£9.99
9780857384331	
WODEHOUSE AT THE WI	£8.99
9780099551362	
Balance to pay	£18.98
Unknown Card	£18.9
8	

Following tender has been voided

Unknown Card	-£18.98
Cash	£20.00
CHANGE	£1.02

- - - - - - - - - - - - - - - - -

THE WATERSTONES CARD
CARD NUMBER: **** **** **** 1246

Your Current Balance	£10.00
Qualifying spend	£18.98
Starting Stamps total	8.5
Stamps earned in this transaction	1
Current Stamps total	9.5

Stamps collected so far on this card

VAT Reg No. GB 108 2770 24

STORE	TILL	OP NO.	TRANS.	DATE	TIME
680	1	816094	903219	17/03/2022	16:06

□999020680001903219□

Waterstones

Refunds & exchanges

We will happily refund or exchange
goods within 30 days or at the manager's
discretion. Please bring them back with
this receipt and in resalable condition.
There are some exclusions such as Book
Tokens and specially ordered items, so
please ask a bookseller for details.

This does not affect your statutory rights.

Waterstone

MCC

In speaking of our cricketers,
    This maxim guideth me,
If they win a match they're 'England',
    If they lose they're 'MCC'.

Under MVC Rules

['A new game called Vigoro has been invented, which combines the characteristics of cricket and lawn-tennis. A trial match has been arranged at Lord's, in which many county players are to take part, and Lord Hawke has announced his intention of introducing it into New Zealand during his forthcoming tour. It can be played all the year round, and, as the ball used is of soft india-rubber, equally well by both sexes. Batsmen, bowlers, and fieldsmen are all armed with racquets.' – *Daily Paper*.]

From the 'Sporting Man' of Dec. 5, 1910.

. . . 'And so ended the first of the five Test matches. We hold no brief for England, but we feel that it cannot be denied that the better side won. Except for an hour on the first day, when Miss Smith and Miss Robinson were at the wickets, the New Zealanders were completely outplayed. And this, in spite of the fact that the luck went dead against the home team from the outset, for with MacLaren unable to turn out, and Miss Jones suffering from acute neuralgia, England was by no means at its full strength. Again, during the majority of the three days snow fell heavily, and it is common knowledge that Lockwood is never at his best on a snowy wicket. Indeed, we seriously question the wisdom of the selection committee in playing him. On his day, it is true, Lockwood is the finest bowler in England. The peculiar twist of his racquet which invariably precedes an off-break is a secret which he shares with no other fast bowler. But since it was obvious from the outset that there would be snow, we think the committee should have given the place to Miss Brown, who rarely fails to do well on any wicket, and is known to have a partiality for the Lord's ground. However, England won. That is the main point, and a victory so decisive will be the most fitting answer to the pessimistic letters which have appeared repeatedly of late in the columns of the Press. Our players may have their off-seasons, but, in view of this victory, it cannot be said with any semblance of reason that English Vigoro is degenerating. The first of the Test-matches has added immensely to the prestige of English Vigoro.

In fielding we still have much to learn from our visitors. The performance of the New Zealanders in England's first innings, and indeed throughout the match, was a treat to behold. Anything finer than the catch by which Miss Slogginson dismissed Gilbert Jessop it has never been our lot to witness. At first sight the hit appeared perfectly safe. The ball had all the well-known force of Mr Jessop's racquet behind it, and, as so often happens with soft india-rubber balls, was swerving nastily. Miss Slogginson, however, though fully thirty yards away, and up to her waist in a deep drift, nevertheless contrived to extricate herself and arrest the ball on her racquet just as it was about to clear the ropes. A wonderful effort, which brought down the house, together with a small avalanche from the roof of the pavilion.

Hirst and Rhodes both appeared a little stale. Playing since January without a break has had its effect on the two Yorkshire cracks, though their deliveries never looked easy. By a curious coincidence each secured his thousandth wicket this season in his first over.

In conclusion we have to thank the committee of the MVC and Ground for their treatment of the press representatives. The new stoves in the press Box are an excellent innovation. We wish we could express equal praise for certain of the other arrangements in force at Lord's. The growing habit of stopping the game at five o'clock for a hot potatoes interval is the curse of modern Vigoro. It annoys the spectators, and is quite unnecessary.

Five Minutes on the Cricket Field

If the number of assistant-under-secretaries of county clubs were placed end to end they would reach from Hyde Park Corner to Peckham Rye.

There is no actual written rule prohibiting a Lancashire man from playing for Lancashire, or a Middlesex man for playing for Middlesex; but it is looked on as rather bad form for them to try.

If all the Surrey skippers skipped simultaneously there would be an earthquake.

The technicalities of cricket occasionally baffle the beginner, who is sometimes puzzled even by the fact that a team touring in Australia is called England when it wins a test match and MCC when it loses.

A cricketer must mount the ladder slowly. It was not till he had played with success for some years that the half-penny papers referred to Rhodes as Wilfred.

Now, Talking About Cricket

In the days of yore, when these white hairs were brown – or was it black? At any rate, they were not white – and I was at school, it was always my custom, when Fate obliged me to walk to school with a casual acquaintance, to whom I could not unburden my soul of those profound thoughts which even then occupied my mind, to turn the struggling conversation to the relative merits of cricket and football.

'Do you like cricket better than footer?' was my formula. Now, though at the time, in order to save fruitless argument, I always agreed with my companion, and praised the game he praised, in the innermost depths of my sub-consciousness, cricket ranked a long way in front of all other forms of sport. I may be wrong. More than once in my career it has been represented to me that I couldn't play cricket for nuts. My captain said as much when I ran him out in *the* match of the season after he had made forty-nine and looked like stopping. A bowling acquaintance heartily endorsed his opinion on the occasion of my missing three catches off him in one over. This, however, I attribute to prejudice, for the man I missed ultimately reached his century, mainly off the deliveries of my bowling acquaintance. I pointed out to him that, had I accepted any one of the three chances, we should have missed seeing the prettiest century made on the ground that season; but he was one of those bowlers who sacrifice all that is beautiful in the game to mere wickets. A sordid practice.

Later on, the persistence with which my county ignored my claims to inclusion in the team, convinced me that I must leave cricket fame to others. True, I did figure, rather prominently, too, in one county match. It was at the Oval, Surrey *v.* Middlesex. How well I remember that occasion! Albert Trott was bowling (Bertie we used to call him); I forget who was batting. Suddenly the ball came soaring in my direction. I was not nervous. I put down the sandwich I was eating, rose from my seat, picked the ball up neatly, and returned it with unerring aim to a fieldsman who was waiting for it with becoming deference. Thunders of applause went up from the crowded ring.

That was the highest point I ever reached in practical cricket. But, as the historian says of Mr Winkle, a man may be an excellent sportsman in theory, even if he fail in practice. That's me. Reader (if any), have you ever played cricket in the passage outside your study with a walking-stick and a ball of paper? That's the game, my boy, for testing the skill of wrist and eye. A century *v.* the MCC is well enough in its way, but give me the man who can watch 'em in a narrow passage, lit only by a flickering gas-jet, – one for every hit, four if it reaches the end, and six if it goes downstairs full-pitch, any pace bowling allowed. To make double figures in such a match is to taste life. Only you had better do your tasting when the housemaster is out for the evening.

I like to watch the young cricket idea shooting. I refer to the lower games, where 'next man in' umpires with his pads on, his loins girt, and a bat in his hand. Many people have wondered why it is that no budding umpire can officiate unless he holds a bat. For my part, I think there is little foundation for the theory that it is part of a semi-religious rite, on the analogy of the Freemason's special handshake and the like. Nor do I altogether agree with the authorities who allege that man, when standing up, needs something as a prop or support. There is a shadow of reason, I grant, in this supposition, but after years of keen observation I am inclined to think that the umpire keeps his bat by him, firstly, in order that no unlicensed hand shall commandeer it unbeknownst, and secondly, so that he shall be ready to go in directly his predecessor is out. There is an ill-concealed restiveness about his movements, as he watches the batsmen getting set, that betrays an overwrought spirit. Then of a sudden one of them plays a ball on to his pad. "'s that?" asks the bowler, with an overdone carelessness. 'Clean out. Now *I'm* in,' and already he is rushing up the middle of the pitch to take possession. When he gets to the wicket a short argument ensues. 'Look here, you idiot, I hit it hard.' 'Rot, man, out of the way.' '!!??!' 'Look here, Smith, *are* you going to dispute the umpire's decision?' Chorus of fieldsmen: 'Get out, Smith, you ass. You've been given out years ago.' Overwhelmed by popular execration, Smith reluctantly departs, registering in the black depths of his soul a resolution to take on the umpireship at once, with a view to gaining an artistic revenge by giving his enemy run out on the earliest possible occasion. There is a primeval *insouciance* about this sort of thing which is as refreshing to a mind jaded with the stiff formality of professional umpires as a cold shower-bath.

I have made a special study of last-wicket men; they are divided into two classes, the deplorably nervous, or the outrageously confident. The nervous largely outnumber the confident. The launching of a last-wicket man, when there are ten to make to win, or five minutes left to make a draw of a losing game, is fully as impressive a ceremony as the launching of the latest battleship. An interested crowd harasses the poor victim as he is putting on his pads. 'Feel in a funk?' asks some tactless friend. 'N-n-no, norrabi.' 'That's right,' says the captain encouragingly, 'bowling's as easy as anything.'

This cheers the wretch up a little, until he remembers suddenly that the captain himself was distinctly at sea with the despised trundling, and succumbed to his second ball, about which he obviously had no idea whatever. At this he breaks down utterly, and, if emotional, will sob into his batting glove. He is assisted down the pavilion steps, and reaches the wickets in a state of collapse. Here, very probably, a reaction will set in. The sight of the crease often comes as a positive relief after the vague terrors experienced in the pavilion.

The confident last-wicket man, on the

other hand, goes forth to battle with a light quip upon his lips. The lot of a last-wicket batsman, with a good eye and a sense of humour, is a very enviable one. The incredulous disgust of the fast bowler, who thinks that at last he may safely try that slow head-ball of his, and finds it lifted genially over the leg-boundary, is well worth seeing. I remember in one school match, the last man, unfortunately on the opposite side, did this three times in one over, ultimately retiring to a fluky catch in the slips with forty-one to his name. Nervousness at cricket is a curious thing. As the author of *Willow the King*, himself a county cricketer, has said, it is not the fear of getting out that causes funk. It is a sort of intangible *je ne sais quoi*. I trust I make myself clear. Some batsmen are nervous all through a long innings. With others the feeling disappears with the first boundary.

A young lady – it is, of course, not polite to mention her age to the minute, but it ranged somewhere between eight and ten – was taken to see a cricket match once. After watching the game with interest for some time, she gave out this profound truth: 'They all attend specially to one man.' It would be difficult to sum up the causes of funk more lucidly and concisely. To be an object of interest is sometimes pleasant, but when ten fieldsmen, a bowler, two umpires, and countless spectators are eagerly watching your every movement, the thing becomes embarrassing.

That is why it is, on the whole, preferable to be a cricket spectator rather than a cricket player. No game affords the spectator such unique opportunities of exerting his critical talents. You may have noticed that it is always the reporter who knows most about the game. Everyone, moreover, is at heart a critic, whether he represent the majesty of the Press or not. From the lady of Hoxton, who crushes her friend's latest confection with the words, 'My! wot an 'at!' down to that lowest class of all, the persons who call your attention (in print) to the sinister meaning of everything Clytemnestra says in the *Agamemnon*, the whole world enjoys expressing an opinion of its own about something.

In football you are vouchsafed fewer chances. Practically all you can do is to shout 'off-side' whenever an opponent scores, which affords but meagre employment for a really critical mind. In cricket, however, nothing can escape you. Everything must be done in full sight of everybody. There the players stand, without refuge, simply inviting criticism.

It is best, however, not to make one's remarks too loud. If you do, you call down upon yourself the attention of others, and are yourself criticised. I remember once, when I was of tender years, watching a school match, and one of the batsmen lifted a ball clean over the pavilion. This was too much for my sensitive and critical young mind. 'On the carpet, sir,' I shouted sternly, well up in the treble clef, 'keep 'em on the carpet.' I will draw a veil. Suffice it to say that I became a sport and derision, and was careful for the future to criticise in a whisper. But the reverse by no means crushed me. Even now I take a melancholy pleasure in watching school matches, and saying So-and-So will make quite a fair *schoolboy* bat in time, but he must get rid of that stroke of his on the off, and that shocking leg-hit, and a few of those *awful* strokes in the slips, but that on the whole, he is by no means lacking in promise. I find it refreshing. If, however, you feel compelled not merely to look on, but to play, as one often does at schools where cricket is compulsory, it is impossible to exaggerate the importance of white boots. The game you play before you get white boots is not cricket, but a weak imitation. The process of initiation is generally this. One plays in shoes for a few years with the most dire results, running away to square leg from fast balls, and so on, till despair seizes the soul. Then an angel in human form (in the very effective disguise of the man at the school boot-shop) hints that, for an absurdly small sum in cash, you may become the sole managing director of a pair of *white buckskin* boots with real spikes. You try them on. They fit, and the initiation is complete. You no longer run away from fast balls. You turn them neatly off to the boundary. In a word, you begin for the first time to play the game, the whole game, and nothing but the game.

There are misguided people who complain that cricket is becoming a business more than a game, as if that were not the most fortunate thing that could happen. When it ceases to be a mere business and becomes a religious ceremony, it will be a sign that the millennium is at hand. The person who regards cricket as anything less than a business is no fit companion, gentle reader, for the likes of you and me. As long as the game goes in his favour the cloven hoof may not show itself. But give him a good steady spell of leather-hunting, and you will know him for what he is, a mere *dilettante*, a dabbler, in a word, a worm, who ought never to be allowed to play at all. The worst of this species will sometimes take advantage of the fact that the game in which they happen to be playing is only a scratch game, upon the result of which no very great issues hang, to pollute the air they breathe with verbal, and the ground they stand on with physical buffooneries. Many a time have I, and many a time have you, if you are what I take you for, shed tears of blood at the sight of such. Careless returns, overthrows, – but enough of a painful subject. Let us pass on.

I have always thought it a better fate for a man to be born a bowler than a bat. A batsman certainly gets a considerable amount of innocent fun by snicking good fast balls *just* off his wicket to the ropes, and standing stolidly in front against slow leg-breaks. These things are good, and help one to sleep peacefully o' nights, and enjoy one's meals. But no batsman can experience that supreme emotion of 'something attempted, something done,' which comes to a bowler when a ball pitches in a hole near point's feet, and whips into the leg stump. It is one crowded second of glorious life. Again, the words 'retired hurt' on the score-sheet are far more pleasant to the bowler than the batsman. The groan of a batsman when a loose ball hits him full pitch in the ribs is genuine. But the 'Awfully-sorry-old-chap-it-slipped' of the bowler is not. Half a loaf is better than no bread, as Mr Chamberlain might say, and if he cannot hit the wicket, he is perfectly contented with hitting the man. In my opinion, therefore, the bowler's lot, in spite of billiard table wickets, red marl, and such like inventions of a degenerate age, is the happier one.

And here, glowing with the pride of originality at the thought that I have written of cricket without mentioning Alfred Mynn or Fuller Pilch, I heave a reminiscent sigh, blot my MS., and thrust my pen back into its sheath.

Dulwich *v.* St Paul's
(1939)

Played at Dulwich, July 8.
Result: St Paul's won by 27 runs.

It is a pity that the threatening weather reduced the crowd watching this match after roll-call to three – or it may have been four – for the school missed thereby a valuable object lesson in how not to bat when faced by a total of 212 on an easy wicket. Our innings lasted exactly 195 minutes, in which time we scored 185 runs. As somebody said, you can't run a business that way.

Oddly enough, this frightful game – probably the dreariest ever seen on the school grounds – started as if we were going to have a bright and exciting day. Mischler and Somper got going briskly, and 71 was on the board when Somper, who had been badly missed at slip by Collingwood and had given a hard c & b chance to Thomas, played outside a good ball from Bailey and was bowled. Walker made some nice shots and Mischler looked like getting a century, when Bailey suddenly produced an unexpected slow one and, following up, took an excellent c & b. Soon afterwards Field caught Brett at the wicket off Knight, Collingwood took Walker at mid-off with a high one-handed catch, and Bailey bowled Mann, the score at that point being 110 for 5. Bailey had bowled splendidly from the start.

What we wanted now was another quick wicket, but Arnold and Rahman settled down, Rahman playing particularly attractively. At 146 he gave an easy c & b to Mallett.

The next wicket added 28. The score was 185 for 8, and the innings finished in a shower of rain for 212, Bailey getting the last man lbw, which made his figures 5 for 41, a fine performance.

Up till now there had been nothing to complain of, except one or two bits of slack fielding, nor did Collingwood and Turner start so badly. Collingwood got a nice four to leg off Dailey's first over, and singles came pretty regularly. Then there were three maidens, after which Turner got a four to leg, followed by a fine off drive to the boundary. Hennessy came on – slow left hand – and Collingwood took a two and a four off successive balls. Looking back in the light of after events, this part of the innings seems like a partnership between Gimblett and H.T. Bartlett. But at 29 Collingwood was stumped off Hennessy, and the timeless Test began.

Even then, there were occasional flashes of brightness. Turner got a couple of fours and Mallett one, and the score was 57 at the end of the first hour. Then Turner called Mallett for an impossible run, and the latter was out by yards, just as he was beginning to show signs of setting about the bowling.

Barnett came in and got a lovely shot past cover to the boundary, and it was after that

that the grim business started. The next ten minutes produced one run, and then Barnett was lbw. This brought Bailey in, and the next twelve minutes saw the pace of scoring quicken. Four runs were added in that period of time. Eventually Turner got a single, which gave him his 50. He then drove a half-volley to the boundary and the 100 went up after an hour and three-quarters.

The next seven minutes brought the score to 101, and then Turner suddenly got two more fours and Bailey a two and a four, and things were looking brighter when Turner was bowled at 130. He had played an innings which can be criticised only for its slowness. He gave no chances and actually hit nine fours.

It now began to dawn on the skipper that at this rate of scoring we had not a hope of making the runs, and he sent Knight in. Knight opened with a fine cut for four, and gave every sign of being about to improve the situation. Unfortunately, he was bowled at 143, and Hammond came in.

Five wickets were now down, but anxiety in the pavilion was entirely confined to the question of whether we could get the runs in the time. It did not seem possible that we could actually be beaten. Hammond did us proud. He – alone on the side – played the right game. He wasted no time, but got going at once with a grand drive to the boundary. Bailey, who had been in a sort of coma for about an hour and twenty minutes, got a four to leg, and Hammond, continuing the good work, followed up a three to leg with a drive for three and another drive for four. Then, just as the happy ending seemed in sight, he was stumped, having played an excellent innings of 17. 175 for 6.

The rest was disaster. The next four wickets added ten runs, and we were beaten at ten minutes to seven.

We would like to add a word of respectful praise for the admirable way in which Mischler captained the St Paul's side in the field. He had not much bowling to help him, but he handled what he had got like a master.

(Reproduced by kind permission of the Master and Governors of Dulwich College)

Extras

P.G. Wodehouse played in one further match serious enough to be recorded (*beyond those mentioned previously*). This was for Bourton Vale against MCC in 1906, at Bourton-on-the-Water in Gloucestershire. Batting No.9 in a 12-a-side match, Plum made three and 24, and took one wicket; MCC won by nine wickets. The Wodehouse link came because his favourite Aunt, Louisa Deane (the model for Aunt Dahlia), lived at Bourton. The club was strongly supported by local landowners and the upper classes, and played a regular fixture against MCC from 1891, as well as entertaining the Eton Ramblers from 1893. A member of the 1906 Bourton Vale team was G.H. Simpson-Hayward, who captained Worcestershire, played five Tests for England in 1909-10, and was the last of the great "lob" (underarm) bowlers in big cricket.

★ ★ ★

The youngest Wodehouse brother, Richard Lancelot Deane, known always as Dick, who was born on May 30, 1892, and went to Cheltenham rather than Dulwich, played three first-class cricket matches while working in India. These were for The Europeans in the Quadrangular Tournament; he batted six times for a total of 84, with a top score of 52 (against the Parsis), and took five wickets for 138 runs.

★ ★ ★

Elder brother Armine might have been forgiven some disillusion with cricket after his most publicised effort for Dulwich in 1898 – his last year at school. Batting No.5 for the college in its major match against MCC, he made a duck in the first innings and six in the second – run out both times.

★ ★ ★

There is a rare slighting Wodehousean reference to cricket in *"Creatures of Impulse"*, published in October, 1914, in *Strand Magazine* and *McClure's*, and reprinted in the Plum Stones series. When the somewhat stuffy and lonely Sir Godfrey Tanner KCMG stayed at the private school run by his nephew George he was bothered by the endless activities and noise of the small boys. Tanner Snr sought solace in the stable yard where, to his nephew's surprise, he was found one day playing cricket "unskilfully, but with extreme energy". Sir Godfrey explains; "I suppose many years ago one would have found pleasure in ridiculous foolery of that sort. It seems hardly credible, but I imagine there was a time when I might really have enjoyed it". On his nephew suggesting, "It's a good game", Sir Godfrey responds; "For children possibly.

Merely for children. However it certainly appears to be capital exercise".

★ ★ ★

"Shall we ever get Bradman out in the Tests?" (Letter from PGW to Bill Townend on May 15, 1938, referring to the series about to begin in England). Answer: Yes – for scores of 51, 18, 103, and 16. He also made 144 not out and 102 not out, while being unable to bat in either innings of the Fifth Test. Average – 108.5.

★ ★ ★

PGW drew his character Claude Cattermole "Catsmeat" Potter-Pirbright from real life, Catsmeat having taken to the stage partly because it allowed him the chance to play county cricket. He was based on Basil Foster of the famous Worcestershire Fosters, whom Plum had met on the cricket field. B.S. Foster opened the innings for Actors against Authors at Lord's in 1907, and made 100 before being caught by A.A. Milne off PGW's bowling. Dismissed for 193 (Plum out for a single), the Authors were then hit for 253 for four wickets off just 26 overs. Plum's 2/36 off five overs were the only reasonable bowling figures. Basil Foster played the hero, George Bevan, in the 1928 New Theatre (London) production of *A Damsel in Distress*, adapted by PGW and Ian Hay from the Wodehouse novel of the same name. He also played Psmith in *Leave It to Psmith* at the Shaftesbury Theatre in 1930.

The cricket-enthused English journalist Michael Davie spent a day at Remsenburg to mark PGW's 90th birthday, resulting in an article in *The Observer* of October 10, 1971. Asked how Bertie Wooster was conjured up, PGW responded: "Bertie was an absolutely recognisable type when I started writing about him. How jolly life was in those days! I was thinking of the country house cricket matches: I played in a lot of them. Everyone seemed to have a reasonable amount of money. I mean, the Berties never had to work". Which country houses staged those matches which Plum enjoyed, you wonder. Are there any scoresheets tucked away in their libraries?

Plum's enthusiasm for Surrey cricket must have been encouraged by the Dulwich professional from 1872 to 1895, William Shepherd. *The Alleynian* declared in 1879, "From the arrival of Shepherd dates a complete reform in the history of our cricket". Shepherd was just 5 ft 5½ inches tall, and weighed a little over nine stone. As a left-arm, medium-pace bowler he had a unique delivery, "which gave the impression he was extracting the ball from his waistcoat pocket". Born in Kennington in 1840, he played 13 matches for Surrey in 1864-65, then making his name as a coach, with engagements at Oxford and The Oval, before joining Dulwich. Shepherd drained, levelled and re-turfed the college playing fields, and devoted enormous energy to the cause of Dulwich cricket.

★ ★ ★

Cricket My Pleasure, the book of memories by
the Yorkshireman A.A. Thomson, was said to
have been read by PGW in one sitting. He
added that it was "the best he had ever come
across".

★ ★ ★

A tribute to Plum's love of cricket came in
1998 with the formation of The Gold Bats, a
team representing The P.G. Wodehouse
Society (UK). Beginning with an annual
match against The Dulwich Dusters – the
Dulwich College masters – this extended its
fixture list in 2001 with the first of a series of
games against The Sherlock Holmes Society
of London, played at West Wycombe under
the Laws of Cricket applying in 1895 (in honour of Holmes's declaration, "It is always
1895"). The Gold Bats now also play regularly against The Charterhouse Intellectuals,
The Kirby Strollers, and The Mount, as well
as contributing members to George
Sherston's XI v Matfield Village, a match
played in memory of Siegfried Sassoon.

★ ★ ★

PGW wrote to Ralph Blumenau, author of *A
History of Malvern College 1865-1965*:
"When I was a small boy, I used to spend
part of the summer holidays with an uncle
who was Vicar of Upton-on-Severn, and I
played a lot of boys' cricket, some of it on
the Malvern ground. From those early days,

the place fascinated me. I was of course cricket-mad, and I can well remember peering in at the pavilion and reading all those illustrious names on the boards". (The author notes; "Malvern cricket was the inspiration [sic] of P.G. Wodehouse's schoolboy story, *Mike at Wrykyn*; the Jackson brothers in that book are taken from the Fosters, and the climax is, appropriately, the 'Ripton Match'").

Acknowledgements

The idea for this book stemmed from a simple question which crystallised in my mind in years of reading Wodehouse: just how good a cricketer was Plum? Might he have got his Blue, perhaps played for a county, if he had gone to Oxford, instead of being thrust into the world of banking?

Sir Edward Cazalet was most helpful in my early inquiries, and approved the initial article I wrote for *Wisden Cricket Monthly*. Tony Ring, who pushed the idea that my original research should be expanded, and provided the introductions necessary to the publishing world, has been a security blanket as well as a catalyst, and an endless source of material. I am much in his debt for his cheery readiness to share the depth of his Wodehouse knowledge, and the range of his remarkable collection.

Colonel Norman Murphy was encouraging and helpful in one vital area, confirming that he had found no detail of Plum's post-Dulwich cricket other than his Authors' appearances – effectively reassuring me that if N.T.P. Murphy had found nothing, then it was improbable that anyone would do so. Barry Phelps also responded swiftly and positively to queries, as did the doyen of them all, Richard Usborne.

Dr Jan Piggott at Dulwich was an essential part of the information team, even if my first visit to his treasure house was made in time of domestic flood (to my heartfelt relief, no Wodehouse documents were affected).

His predecessor, Margaret Slythe, also had helpful thoughts to offer and made most encouraging comments.

Old Alleynian Trevor Bailey (humorously resigned to being quizzed yet again about the notorious description of his batting against St Paul's in 1939) and his old skipper A.C. Shirreff, who expanded on Plum's delight at the Eleven's 1938 unbeaten run, were appreciated on-the-spot witnesses.

Mike Griffith was kind in explaining his relationship as Wodehouse's godson, who inherited his Christian name from Wodehouse's greatest cricketing character.

Michelle Simpson was much appreciated for providing copies of the *Public School Magazine*, once we found our way to the A & C Black archives in the delightful village of Eaton Soken.

David Rayvern Allen produced an invaluable file of *Punch* material on cricket stemming from his own researches, and a welcome Wodehouse letter to John Arlott.

David Frith as ever was interested in something beyond the normal pattern of cricket writing, to give my preliminary article welcome exposure in *Wisden Cricket Monthly*.

MCC curator Stephen Green and his colleagues were helpful as always in pointing me in the right direction in the Lord's collection, not least in producing a forgotten picture of Wodehouse in 1902, with The Authors XI.

Richard Morris and David Moriarty of the Wodehouse Society were encouraging, while Frits Menschaar, New York collector, dealer and enthusiast, proved that Americans can indeed have a true feeling for cricket with his helpful thoughts and detail.

John Hayward, Yorkshire-born secretary of the Hollywood Cricket Club, was a cheerful collaborator in checking Wodehouse links with that happy band of exiles – but alas, could find no proof that Plum ever actually donned flannels in the States.

Sir Donald Bradman was courteous and kindly as he always is to his vast network of correspondents, responding promptly to my inquiry whether he had met Plum with the touring Australian cricket team in Los Angeles in 1932.

My family was indulgent as its various members have always been about my highways and byways of enthusiasms: my wife Petra, one of those people who found Wodehouse in youth but no longer read him, made all the right responses when I needed encouragement or motivation, as she has done throughout so many rewarding years together.

And Tony Whittome at Hutchinson was sympathetically and breezily persuasive and helpful throughout an old newspaper hand's introduction to the mysterious new world of book publishing.

Actors v. Authors.

THURSDAY, JUNE 29.

AUTHORS.	First Innings.		Second Innings.
1 Sir A. Conan Doyle	b Warner	2	
2 P. G. Wodehouse, Esq...	b Smith	0	
3 Cecil Headlam, Esq......	b Smith	9	
4 J. C. Snaith, Esq..........	c Denbigh, b O'Connor ..	17	
5 A. Kinross, Esq.	b Smith	5	
6 Horace Bleakley, Esq....	not out	54	
7 C. C. Hoyer Millar, Esq.	b Denbigh	3	
8 Major Philip Trevor......	b Warner	44	
9 Leo Trevor, Esq.	b Warner	4	
10 E. W. Hornung, Esq. ...			
11 P. Graves, Esq............	[Innings closed.]		
12 F. Stayton, Esq.			

	B 5, l-b 3, w 2, n-b 1, 11	B , l-b , w , n-b ,
	Total 149	Total ......,.............. ...

BOWLING ANALYSIS.

Name.	O.	1st Innings.						2nd Innings.				
		M.	R.	W.	Wds.	N-b.	O.	M.	R.	W.	Wds.	N-b.
O'Connor	10	5	28	1	..	..	..	..	..	..	..	..
Smith	11	1	39	3	..	..	..	..	..	..	..	..
Warner	9	0	24	3	2	..	..	..	..	..	..	..
Denbigh....................	7	0	23	1	..	..	..	..	..	..	..	..
Evett	3	0	10	0	..	..	..	..	..	..	..	..
Asche	4	1	14	0	..	1	..	..	..	..	..	..

ACTORS.	First Innings.		Second Innings.
1 V. O'Connor, Esq..........	not out 100		
2 H. B. Warner, Esq.	b Wodehouse...............	6	
3 Reeve Denbigh, Esq......	b Millar	21	
4 C. Aubrey Smith, Esq...	c Wodehouse, b Millar...	9	
5 Gerald Du Maurier, Esq.	not out	13	
6 A. S. Homewood, Esq....			
7 Oscar Asche, Esq.			
8 Robert Evett, Esq.			
9 P. F. Knox, Esq.			
10 H. Nye Chart, Esq.			
11 Kenneth Douglas, Esq...			
12 C. Hayden Coffin, Esq...			

	B 3, l-b 3, w , n-b 1, 7	B , l-b , w , n-b ,
	Total 156	Total ....

BOWLING ANALYSIS.

Name.	O.	1st Innings.						2nd Innings.				
		M.	R.	W.	Wds.	N-b.	O.	M.	R.	W.	Wds.	N-b.
Snaith	4	1	16	0	..	..	..	..	..	..	..	..
Doyle	8	1	45	0	..	1	..	..	..	..	..	..
Wodehouse	10	0	58	1	..	..	..	..	..	..	..	..
Millar.......................	6	0	30	2	..	..	..	..	..	..	..	..

Umpires—Pougher and Brown.   Scorers—Martin and Atfield.

Actors won by 7 wickets and 7 runs.

(Lord's, 1905: by permission of MCC)

Authors v. Publishers.

TUESDAY, AUGUST 22.

PUBLISHERS.	First Innings.	Second Innings.
1 W. Cutbush	c Croome, b Doyle 0	
2 W. Farquharson	c Selincourt, b Doyle ... 0	
3 R. Truslove	b Wodehouse 27	
4 A. G. Agnew ..	b Wodehouse 82	
5 A. C. Dene	b Thurston................... 60	
6 L. E. G. Abney	b Wodehouse 19	
7 W. Longman	b Wodehouse 5	
8 S. S. Pawling	run out 0	
9 E. Fagg	c Croome, b Thurston ... 8	
10 F. J. Harvey Darton ...	st Croome, b Thurston... 24	
11 H. H. Thomas	not out 5	
	B 4, l-b 2, w 4, n-b , 10	B , l-b , w , n-b ,
	Total 240	Total ....

BOWLING ANALYSIS. Name.	O.	1st Innings. M.	R.	W.	Wds.	N-b.	2nd Innings. O.	M.	R.	W.	Wds.	N-b.
Doyle	13	4	88	2	..	..	..	..	..	..	..	..
Selincourt	7	1	28	0	..	..	..	..	..	..	..	..
Irwin	7	1	87	0	1	..	..	..	..	..	..	..
Croome	9	1	23	0	2	..	..	..	..	..	..	..
Wodehouse	20	3	75	4	..	..	..	..	..	..	..	..
Thurston	4.3	0	16	3	..	..	..	..	..	..	..	..
Scott	2	0	13	0	1	..	..	..	..	..	..	..

AUTHORS.	First Innings.	Second Innings.
1 R. B. J. Scott	b Thomas 24	
2 A. Worsley	c Pawling, b Cutbush ... 75	
3 A. C. M. Croome	c and b Thomas 0	
4 P. G. Wodehouse	c Pawling, b Cutbush ... 60	
5 Sir A. Conan Doyle	b Pawling 14	
6 W. Livingstone Irwin ...	c Cutbush, b Pawling ... 6	
7 E. Temple Tharston......	c Dene, b Longman 10	
8 Hugh de Selincourt	c and b Longman 7	
9 Gunby Hadath.............	not out 5	
10 G. C. Ives	not out 1	
11 John Barnett		
	B 11, l-b 5, w , n-b , 16	B , l-b , w , n-b ,
	Total 218	Total ....

BOWLING ANALYSIS. Name.	O.	1st Innings. M.	R.	W.	Wds.	N-b.	2nd Innings. O.	M.	R.	W.	Wds.	N-b.
Longman	19	4	63	2	..	..	..	..	..	..	..	..
Cutbush	10	2	39	2	..	..	..	..	..	..	..	..
Abney	3	0	17	0	..	..	..	..	..	..	..	..
Pawling	11	1	40	2	..	.	..	..	..	..	..	..
Thomas	9	1	29	2	..	..	..	..	..	..	..	..
Farquharson	4	1	14	0	..	..	..	..	..	..	..	..

Umpires—Atfield and Whiteside.　　　　Scorers—Storer and Attewell.

Drawn.

(Lord's, 1911: by permission of MCC)

The scorecard of the match between Dulwich Modern VI and Remove, in which Wodehouse took nine wickets (by kind permission of the Master and Governors of Dulwich College)

The Dulwich Classical VI cricket XI, 1900. Wodehouse is seated on the left of the captain. Reproduced by kind permission of the Master and Governors of Dulwich College.

Authors v. Artists, Esher, May 1903. (By permission of MCC)

The Hollywood Cricket Club, 1945/6. C. Aubrey Smith
bats while Boris Karloff threatens behind the stumps
(by permission of Sussex County CC)